PERFORMERS
AND
PLAYERS

PERFORMERS AND PLAYERS

by
Irene M. Franck
and
David M. Brownstone

A Volume in the Work Throughout History Series

Facts On File®
New York · Oxford

Library of Congress Cataloging-in-Publication Data

Franck, Irene M.
  Performers and players.

  (Work throughout history series)
  Bibliography: p.
  1. Performing arts—History—Juvenile literature.
2. Entertainers—Vocational guidance—Juvenile
literature. 3. Sports—History—Juvenile literature.
4. Athletes—Vocational guidance—Juvenile literature.
I. Brownstone, David M. II. Title.
PN1580.F68 1988 790.2'09 87-30340
ISBN O-8160-1443-4

Printed in the United States of America

10 9 8 7 6 5 4 3 2 1

Composition by Facts On File

Contents

Titles in the *Work Throughout History* series

Preface

Performers and Players is a book in the multi-volume series, *Work Throughout History*. Work shapes the lives of all human beings; yet surprisingly little has been written about the history of the many fascinating and diverse types of occupations men and women pursue. The books in the *Work Throughout History* series explore humanity's most interesting, important, and influential occupations. They explain how and why these occupations came into being in the major cultures of the world, how they evolved over the centuries, especially with changing technology, and how society's view of each occupation has changed. Throughout we focus on what it was like to do a particular kind of work—for example, to be a farmer, glassblower, midwife, banker, building contractor, actor, astrologer, or weaver—in centuries past and right up to today.

Because many occupations have been closely related to one another, we have included at the end of each article references to other overlapping occupations. In preparing this series, we have drawn on a wide range of general works on social, economic, and occupational history, including many on everyday life throughout history. We consulted far too many wide-ranging works to list them all here; but at the end of each volume is a list of suggestions for further reading, should readers want to learn more about any of the occupations included in the volume.

Many researchers and writers worked on the preparation of this series. For *Performers and Players*, the primary researcher-writer was David G. Merrill. Our thanks go to him for his fine work; to our expert typists, Shirley Fenn, Nancy Fishelberg, and Mary Racette; to our most helpful editors at Facts On File, first Kate Kelly and then James Warren, and their assistants Claire Johnston and later Barbara Levine; to our excellent developmental editor, Vicki Tyler; and to our publisher, Edward Knappman, who first suggested the *Work Throughout History* series and has given us gracious support during the long years of its preparation.

We also express our special appreciation to the many librarians whose help has been indispensable in completing this work, especially to the incomparable staff of the Chappaqua Library—director Mark Hasskarl and former director Doris Lowenfels; the reference staff, including Mary Platt, Paula Peyraud, Terry Cullen, Martha Alcott, Carolyn Jones, and formerly Helen Barolini, Karen Baker, and Linda Goldstein; Jane McKean and Marcia Van Fleet and the whole circulation staff—and the many other librarians who, through the Interlibrary Loan network, have provided us with the research tools so vital to our work.

Irene M. Franck
David M. Brownstone

Introduction

Performers and players are some of the most envied people in the world. What other people do for play, as amateurs, they are able to do for pay, as professionals. Whether acting in a play or playing in a baseball game, these people are able to work as professionals because they have an admirable level of skill, which sets them apart from most other performers or players. So, despite the uncertainties and sometimes even dangers of the life, amateurs by the thousands dream of becoming professional performers and players.

Today performers and players work both for their own satisfaction and for the entertainment of others. But thousands of years ago, their work was also closely related to religion, the heart of early society. In many cultures, singing, dancing, athletic feats, and other such activities were all closely linked with service to the gods. Only later did each of these activities branch off to follow a separate line of development.

Drama, music, and dance were all closely linked in the early cultures of the Mediterranean world and Asia. They would remain so in places like China and India, where the three activities have remained combined into modern times. In Western civilization, they began to separate in Greece, where the *actor* first became a major and independent artist. Song and movement remained important, of course, but the play—and the actor—was the thing for the Greeks. The Romans, however, preferred spectacle and a mix of entertainments, so *variety performers* were popular in much of the Roman Empire. These two closely related types of players—the actor and the variety performer—continued to exist side by side in Europe into modern times. Along with these have been the *puppeteers*, who have brought their very special art to audiences throughout the West and especially in the East.

With the flowering of the theater in modern times, and then the coming of movies, radio, and television, celebrity and riches have come to the most successful of actors. Less successful actors, as always, continue to struggle along, living hand-to-mouth, for the chance to continue practicing their art. The actors' poorer cousins, the variety performers, have also achieved fame and success in some measure. The vaudeville and music hall, and most of all the circus, gave them ample fame and material rewards from the public.

Musicians, too, have a long history. They have often worked closely with religious institutions. But many worked outside the religious world, traveling from castle to castle, manor to manor, town to town. *Minstrels, troubadors*, and their kin brought with them tales of the outside world, set to music and sung, or played, for a public starved for both news and entertainment.

In modern times, especially from the 17th century on, musicians—though often underpaid and uncertain about their futures—were sometimes the darlings of Western society. Great *composers, instrumentalists*, and *singers* were wined, dined, and honored as celebrities. As modern technology has spread their talents wider, some modern musicians have become extraordinarily rich and famous.

Some *dancers*, too, have become great stars in modern times. In 17th-century Europe, dancing—which had been largely an amateur activity—began to be performed by professionals, people with skill enough to entertain and please a discriminating audience. While *ballet dancers* were the most popular and successful in that era, in the 20th century, free-form *modern dancers* have joined them in the limelight.

Large and complex productions—theater, music, dance, or any combination of the three—require coordination by a single, unifying mind. That is the work of the *director*, in music called a *conductor*, and in dance, a *choreographer*. Often a performer will perform a double role, acting and directing, for example, or dancing and choreographing. In the modern era, the director is an essential part of any large-scale performance.

Like actors, *athletes* are people who perform both for their own satisfaction and for the entertainment of others. They, too, started in close association with religion. Fine athletic performance—even those involving competition, as in the early Greek Olympic Games—were dedicated to the pleasure of the gods. Athletics also served more practical functions, since they helped keep a country's citizens fit and ready for war, which might come at any time. Indeed, competitive games between nations—then, as now—were often seen almost as a harmless alternative to war.

Early athletics tended to stress individual competition. Today *racers* of various sorts—often using a horse or other vehicle in their competition—are among the many types of athletes continuing that tradition. But in modern times team sports have come to the fore. Team sports were often frowned upon in earlier times. Medieval and

Renaissance rulers often complained that people were playing "futball" rather than practicing important and necessary military skills, such as archery. Today's professional team athletes have become enormously popular, achieving fame and pay undreamt of by athletes of an earlier, simpler time.

Among the millions of people who play the various sports as amateurs, many would dearly love to become professionals. *Sports managers* and *recruiters* have become important figures in identifying and preparing promising players for professional sports. *Athletic coaches* and *trainers* help such hopeful and practicing athletes make the most of their skills. And *sports officials*, such as *referees* and *umpires*, help to ensure that the games are played fairly and by the rules.

Many performers and players face an uncertain life. Often they do not know where they will be working next and for whom. Though actors and musicians often have long working lives, many performers and players have extremely short careers. Athletes and dancers especially have severe physical limits on how long they can exercise their talents as professionals. Some of them face the danger of severe injuries in their work, which may leave them crippled or in pain for the rest of their lives. Even so, the attraction of the careers is so great that children—and adults, too—still dream of becoming professional performers and players, of being honored and paid for doing what they love to do.

Actors

The actor's art has existed for some thousands of years, at first as participation in ritual. It is old, as old as *mimesis*, the imitation and representation of nature. Like the dance, with which it was long intertwined, it is essential to religious practice and is part of religious and political leadership, in our time as it has been throughout what we know of human history.

Some of the surviving Paleolithic art from the period 35,000-10,000 B.C. portrays human figures who may be engaged in ritual. At Coqul, in Spain, for example, a painting shows nine human figures, possibly female, who may be dancing around a single figure, possibly male. At the cave of Trois Frères, in France, a single figure, apparently a human wearing an animal mask or headdress, is portrayed. From these and other such representations have flowed considerable conjecture as to the role of dance and acting in early human rituals. However, acting has become a profession only in the last few thousand years.

The separate but related civilizations of ancient Mesopotamia and ancient Egypt may have been the cradles of the acting profession, but the evidence is so far inconclusive. In Ur, between 3,000 and 2,000 B.C., highly formalized religious observances were held, including processions much like pageants, especially to celebrate the New Year. In Babylon, between 2,000 and 1,000 B.C., a great deal of pageantry required considerable exercise of acting and dancing skills, but no evidence yet indicates that such skills were held to be a special profession or trade.

Much evidence exists of ancient Egyptian rituals dating as far back as the 25th century B.C. A surviving body of ritual text, called the *Pyramid Texts*, consists of writings on the inside walls of pyramids. Some of these texts appear to be "playable" religious dramas, though this assumption is disputed. Ikhernofet, a court official of ancient Egypt, described one such text, the *Abydos Passion Play*, as having been "played" for almost 40 years, between 1887 and 1849 B.C. The play, which has unfortunately not survived, dealt with the death and dismemberment of the god Osiris, and his reassembly by his wife, Isis, and son, Horus. Some historians have guessed that the *Abydos Passion Play* is but the tip of an iceberg. They believe that highly formalized drama-dance employing professional theater people existed in Egyptian culture during this period, and that *performers* worked in many productions. But the available evidence can lead only to conjecture at this time.

As archaeologists and historians learn more of human history, conjecture may turn into knowledge. It seems appropriate to hypothesize that people were practicing the profession of acting long before the Greek Golden Age. But, as of this writing, that is where hard knowledge of the acting profession begins: in the sixth century B.C. in Greece.

Greek Actors

The first professional *actor* we know is Thespis. The term *thespian* is derived from his name. A native of Icaria, in Attica, he spent most of his life as a *poet-dramatist*, creating and touring in performance of his own *dithyrambs* (literally, goat-songs, celebrating the god Dionysus) and the works of others. In performance, other touring *poets* of the time used *narrator, chorus*, and musical instruments. But they did not use actors playing roles. Thespis is best remembered for an extraordinary innovation: He introduced—and probably was himself—the first professional actor. That is, he moved from the role of narrator to that of *impersonator*, or actor, taking any and all of the roles in his own dramas.

Performing artists had worked in Greece long before actors appeared, of course. Greek touring companies—the direct ancestors of the touring companies that have characterized Western theater for nearly 3,000 years—appeared as early as the eighth and ninth centuries B.C., with such performers as *dancers, mimes, acrobats*, and *jugglers* working in the popular arts. These performers were to provide skilled people for all the later theater forms.

Aristotle, in the *Poetics*, attributes the origin of Greek tragedy to improvised stories (*dithyrambs*) sung and danced in homage to Dionysus. The Corinthian poet Arion, near the turn of the sixth century B.C., is credited with being the first to write such dithyrambs, converting them into the tragic form.

Thespis and the acting profession appear on the world stage in 534 B.C., winning the prize for drama at the city of Dionysia, where the Athenian tyrant Pisistratus organized an annual festival of drama. The Dionysiac festivals were held in late March or early April, and were celebrated in many Greek cities. The work that won the prize has been lost, as have all of Thespis' works. What remains is his innovation, the introduction of the actor.

Other dramatist-actors succeeded Thespis in the sixth

century. All of their performances consisted of a single actor—almost always themselves—chorus, and narrator. Phrynichus, near the turn of the century, is credited with introducing the first women's roles. These were, however, invariably played by men, as would continue to be true in all the dramas of ancient Greece.

Aeschylus, a playwright of the early fifth century B.C., introduced a second actor into Greek drama, the roles thereafter being shared by the two actors. He is one of the three great Greek tragedians whose works survive—though all but seven of his approximately 80 plays were lost. Sophocles, writing at the peak of the fifth-century B.C. Greek Golden Age, in the Athens of Pericles and the Athenian Empire, worked ultimately in the fully formed Greek theater. He introduced a third actor, and reduced the size of the tragic chorus from as many as 50 to a number variously reported as 12 or 15. (It was 24 in comedy.) In his work, Sophocles stressed the development of character, and the action that flows from character.

Sophocles is also reported to have been the first to use painted scenery. The term *scene* derives from the Greek word *skēnē*, which was the actors' dressing or changing room. This was located at the back of the floor on which the work was performed, called the *orchēstra*, from which the modern orchestra area of a theater derives its name. The first painted backdrops used on stage were painted on the walls of the *skēnē*. Later, revolving backdrops were developed. Their change probably announced what we would now call a new *scene*.

On the Greek stage, the main actors after the sixth century B.C. were professionals, unless they were primarily dramatists, as was Sophocles. They worked in rather splendid "street clothes," costumes similar in style to ordinary dress, but considerably embellished. They wore masks that entirely covered face and head, changing masks as they changed characters. The leading actor (*protagonist*) took the leading or title roles; the second actor (*deuteragonist*) took the secondary roles, often several of them; and the third actor (*tritagonist*) took all the minor roles. In tragedy, chorus members occasionally played very minor roles, supplementing the work of the three actors. In comedy, there were sometimes more than three actors on stage, although actors in comedy also played multiple roles. In the fully formed Greek theater, all were professionals, paid by the state, supplied to the appropriate festivals to play the roles.

In the sixth and fifth centuries B.C., the members of the chorus were amateurs, led and recruited by the chief choral narrator, the *chorequs*. He was himself an amateur, usually a wealthy local citizen, who paid for the privilege of leading the chorus. In later times, chorus members were professionals; they were described in some works as members of the actors' guilds of the fourth and later centuries. In those later periods, they took rigorous formal training, and functioned essentially as professional actors playing specific roles on stage.

Greek actors enjoyed extraordinary prestige and official community standing—standing not to be matched by any other actors in the Western theater until the late 19th century. Starting in the fourth century B.C., they organized guilds, which included other theater people, such as dramatists, *musicians, costumers*, and *voice teachers*. As their status grew over the course of many decades, these players became a favored group, immune from military service and, in most circumstances, from arrest as well. They traveled widely to perform, even between warring states, and to many foreign countries, as the Greek theater achieved wider popularity.

Actors, and especially those playing in the larger cities, performed in enormous theaters packed with people. The temple of Dionysus, in Athens, the premier Greek theater, started as a vantage point from which to view early dramatic presentations from the hillside below the Acropolis. By the fifth century, it was a major theater, seating as many as 15,000 to 17,000 people. During the third century, it became a permanent stone theater in the same location, on the south slope of the Acropolis. Nor was it alone in its size. Every Greek city had a substantial theater, and the theaters were extremely well attended.

Working in huge theaters without the modern technology of sound amplification, Greek actors' first objective was simply to be heard. They spoke through masks, which may have acted to some extent as megaphones, but may also in some instances have distorted and limited projection. They had to play effectively to large numbers of people in outdoor theaters, often in dramas in which the words were the essence of the work, as was true in Sophocles' plays, for example. Given those circumstances, it is easy to hypothesize that they worked very "large"—that is, in declamatory style and using body language that could be easily perceived by every member of their huge audiences.

For them, the ultimate test was the voice. The actor's voice had to be extraordinarily well trained. It had to be a voice capable of speaking and singing poetry in perfect Athenian Greek and in the style the creators of the work had intended. And, while doing so, the voice had to fill a huge amphitheater with sound. In use and stage function the Greek actor's chief instrument, his voice, was much like the voice of the modern singer in grand opera. In training, in presentation, in relationship with

Thalia, the Muse of Comedy (seated), and Melpomene, The Muse of Tragedy, display the traditional masks worn by early Greek actors. (From Museum of Antiquity, by L.W. Yaggy and T.L. Haines, 1882)

audience, the parallels are striking—as would seem so evident to the Italian neoclassicists who founded the modern Western opera two thousand years after the Greek Golden Age.

The Greek actor's art flourished in Greece for two centuries. Aristotle, writing the *Poetics* during the mid-fourth century B.C., was then seeing a living theater, featuring a large number of rigorously trained actors playing in many great roles after some hundreds of years of the development of their national theater. This was the Greece of Demosthenes, later of Alexander the Great of Macedon. And it was the actor-oriented theater of Polus, Theodorus, Aristodemus, and Thesselus playing the great works of Aeschylus, Sophocles, Euripides, Aristophanes, and scores of other dramatists, so few of whose works have survived.

After Alexander the Great died, in 323 B.C., Greek theater fell into a period of decline, and so did standards of performance in the Greek theater. But Greek actors continued to be the great actors of the ancient Mediterranean world. Although the political focus of the Western world shifted to Rome for a thousand years, Greek actors and other performers continued to play throughout the eastern Mediterranean, as well as in Rome itself.

Roman Actors

Actors in Rome worked in a theater originating in three quite different traditions. The first, and probably dominant, tradition stemmed from the festival theater of Etruria, which predated Rome as a major power on the Italian peninsula and even ruled Rome in some periods before the establishment of the Roman Republic in 509 B.C. Etruria was a major imperial state, stretching to the north of Rome, and contemporary with the emerging states of the Dorian Greeks. Its inhabitants, the Etruscans, introduced the *stadium*, their circus form, and early drama-dance into Rome some hundreds of years before the introduction of the Greek theater.

The second, and related, tradition is that of the Atellan farce. This was a popular *mime* or playlet form developed in the southern Italian city of Atella. These featured several stock characters in a rustic setting. The Atellan farces seem to have been much like the forms later developed by the *commedia dell'arte*, a vastly popular rural farce played in Italy 2,000 years later. No direct lines of influence between them are currently provable, however.

These two forms together merged to develop the characteristically Roman variety theater, in which acting, as the Greeks originated it, occupied only a small part. In the Etruscan, southern Italian, and then Roman theaters, actors worked in variety and carnival settings, in professional companies that were more like circus companies than groups of touring actors. They performed side by side with *jugglers, sword-swallowers, animal trainers, dancers, athletes*, and other such variety performers. Actors in the Roman theater ultimately worked in tragedy, comedy, and popular farce; in speaking roles, as featured singers, as nonspeaking *mimes*, and as balletic *pantomimists*.

The third tradition was that of the Greek theater, to some extent transplanted and adapted to Roman conditions. The early Greeks had established city-states in many parts of the Mediterranean, including the Italian peninsula. The expanding Romans took over these colonies by mid-third century B.C. But through the Greeks who remained under Roman rule, the people of Italy became exposed to Greek drama. The Greek-born poet, *teacher*, and actor, Livius Andronicus, introduced Greek drama and comedy into Rome in 240 B.C., soon after the Romans had completed their conquest of the Greek cities.

Soon the Romans began to imitate the Greeks throughout the arts. By the beginning of the second century B.C., many Greek plays were being translated and adapted for performance in Rome. Roman dramatists were also beginning to write on Roman themes, especially in comedy. The theater so born derived very much from the Greek, and never even began to approach the extraordinary achievements of the Greek theater. But it did flourish as a theater in which professional actors worked for nearly a thousand years.

The nature of the Roman theater changed as Rome changed. During the 150 to 200 years after the introduction of Greek theater, Rome was an expanding republic discovering the treasures of Greek culture. Roman dramatists such as Andronicus and Naevius produced both tragedies and comedies; they were succeeded by such writers of comedies as Plautus and Terence, some of whose works survive.

But as the Roman Republic changed, so did the audience. By the beginning of the first century B.C., very few comedies were being written for production. By 29 B.C., the date of the fall of the Roman Republic and the beginning of the Roman Empire, no tragedies were being written for production. The Roman audience had

To be heard in vast theaters like this one at Pompeii, Classical actors used their masks somewhat like megaphones. (From Das Theater, *by Andreas Streit, 1903)*

developed a taste for spectacle, for star performers, for the circuses developed out of the dominant strain in the Roman theater. These were carefully cultivated by Rome's politicians in the latter days of the republic, and throughout the history of the empire. In the waning days of the republic, the leading figures in the theater were actors, such as Roscius and Aesopus. But by the early years of the first century A.D., the Roman theater was entirely a variety theater, with mimes and pantomimists replacing the actors who had worked in the Greek tradition during the last two and one-half centuries of the republic. The Atellan farce, which remained popular, was based on improvisation, until the first century B.C. Then short written pieces replaced improvisation, and in the next century this type of theater lost much of its popularity, being replaced by circus and pantomime.

Aside from the companies of touring variety players, Roman actors worked in very large outdoor theaters, as had the Greeks before them. They worked in masks, as well, for both the Etruscan and Greek theaters used masks. Like the Greeks, Roman actors faced the need to fill huge performing places with their voices and to work "large."

In the Roman theater, as in the Greek, actors often "doubled," changing masks as they changed roles, but no fixed number of actors was used on stage. Except in mime—in which some women during the later years of the empire became stars—all acting roles were played by men. Although Livius Andronicus was both a dramatist and actor, he was an exception. The main Roman tradition was that of the professional acting company, with the dramatist not working as an actor. In the Roman theater, it was the *manager*, sometimes an *actor-manager*, who was the dominant force.

The professional acting companies they managed were often composed wholly or largely of *slaves*, many of them Greeks. Some students of the Roman theater believe that all Roman players were slaves, while other scholars claim that some prominent actors were freeborn. As the drama eroded, more and more theater presentations were built around scenes and performances designed to show off individual performers. Many pantomimists were soloists, playing with supporting musicians and dancers, but as recognized stars and sometimes superstars of the Roman theater. One pantomimist, Theodora, even married the emperor Justinian in the sixth century A.D.

Even though some performers became soloists and even "stars," the status of actors and other theater people in Rome was generally very low indeed, and worsened as republic gave way to empire. In the early centuries of the Christian era, Roman acting companies were variety show companies, including actors playing in mimes and as pantomimists along with many other additional Etruscan-Roman variety performers.

The Early Christian era

With the rise of Christianity, which became the Roman state religion in 393 A.D., the Roman acting profession came under sharp attack. The Christians did their utmost to destroy the theater. Actors who refused to give up their profession were denied the sacraments, and Christians who attended the secular theater were excommunicated—that is, cut off from the church. Despite this, actors continued to work in the theater. And audiences, although somewhat smaller, continued to attend theatrical productions.

In Europe the acting profession did not survive the periodic invasions of Rome. It held on through most of the sixth century A.D. But after that it could not survive in its previous form. So actors in Western Europe took to the "road" for some centuries.

The Roman Empire had, in 395 A.D., split into two halves: Western and Eastern. The Emperor Constantine, who first made Christianity the official religion of the Roman Empire, had founded a new eastern capital, Constantinople (earlier called Byzantium, today called

Istanbul). Actors in the Eastern Roman Empire (later called the Byzantine Empire) were luckier than their Western counterparts, for there the Roman theater and the acting profession continued. These actors worked in the variety theater, as mimes and pantomimists, along with dancers, acrobats, jugglers, and other variety artists. They worked mainly in Greek, and in a theater composed of many companies, as in Rome. Actors traveled the empire to perform, as they had been doing for 2,000 years.

In Western Europe, nine centuries passed between the fall of Rome and the revival of the theater as part of the Renaissance. This period was in most respects a barren one for professional actors. With the medieval Catholic Church becoming powerful, secular entertainments were discouraged, and professional actors and other theater people were excommunicated. Only in the popular arts did professional actors survive, as members of touring troupes of variety performers. Touring troupes performed at rural festivals, in towns, and wherever a popular audience could be found that was not too heedful of the warnings of the Catholic clergy. Such audiences were to be found throughout Western Europe, especially in those areas where the tradition of the Roman popular variety theater was remembered. In this most difficult of all periods for the theater, actors continued to pursue their profession.

Even within the Catholic Church, the impulse to dramatize developed theater and actors to play it. The religious festivals developed by the church to replace the "pagan" festivals of pre-Christian Europe ultimately became complex pageants. These were not unlike the holiday processions of Mesopotamia and Egypt thousands of years earlier. They were then elaborated further into religious drama, starting in the 10th century A.D. These dramas were staged using amateurs, usually members of the religious orders, but they were precursors of the resurgence of the professional theater that was to come later.

Revival

By the 14th century, the groundwork was being laid for the Renaissance. Feudalism was declining, new nation-states were forming, towns were growing, universities were developing, and Western European commerce and industry were beginning to flourish. A new audience for the theater was beginning to emerge. Under these conditions, the religious drama moved out of the churches, was increasingly presented in vernacular (popular) languages rather than in Latin, and began to use actors who were not members of religious orders. Productions became far more complex. As a result, the professional manager, sometimes an actor-manager, reappeared on the European stage. The actors continued to be amateurs, but as the number of productions increased and their complexity grew, some actors began to be paid, and relatively well, becoming at least semiprofessionals. And some began to be paid as *coaches*, further signaling the revival of the profession.

The secular theater also revived, starting in the 13th century. The popular variety troupes had been the refuge of the professional actor in the West after the fall of Rome. In the later medieval period, from about the 11th to the 15th centuries, actors were often called *minstrels*, and acting troupes combined music, dance, and acting without differentiation between the kinds of performers. The troupes themselves often were adopted by influential patrons, and were officially attached to royal and noble courts, both performing for their patrons and working as troupes traveling under the patrons' protection. Only in the 15th century did differentiation begin to develop between speaking and singing actors in the Western European theater.

Gradually these troupes began attracting dramatists writing for the theater, laying the basis for the development of a new popular theater. In France, England, Germany, and the Low Countries, actors performed in drama, farce, mime, and in the morality plays, such as

Strolling players like these brought their entertainments to the courts of kings and princes throughout Europe. (From Frank Leslie's Popular Monthly Magazine)

the turn-of-the-16th-century English play, *Everyman*, that would lead to the dramas of the Renaissance. These were professional actors, not amateurs or semiprofessionals, but the inheritors of a theatrical tradition going back to Thespis and Sophocles. And, for the first time since before the fall of the Roman Republic, they were working in newly written dramas, playing complete works in ensemble rather than as individual variety performers, and speaking lines.

The 16th century brought the great split in the Catholic Church called the Reformation. In this period, religious drama was banned by both sides—by the Protestant rulers one by one, starting with Elizabeth I of England on her accession to power in 1558, and by the Roman Catholic Church during the Council of Trent, which ended in 1563. By 1600, the only major European country officially permitting religious plays was Spain.

Secular Theater

The theater that remained was wholly secular. The people of the theater were therefore independent professional artists playing for pay. Many troupes continued to be sponsored by the nobility. Financing, playing space, and performance were often a matter of state grants and licenses. But the theater of the late 16th and early 17th centuries—notably in England, Italy, Spain, and France—began to include highly professional actors and acting companies.

In Italy, the actors of the *commedia dell'arte* developed an "actor's theater" very much like that of the Atellan theater of 2,000 years earlier. Featuring a number of stock characters playing professionally in ensemble, these improvisational theaters worked without fully written scripts. They did, however, use hundreds of very specific stock situations, and many scenes were repeated so often that many of the lines and movements supposedly "improvised" on stage were actually taken whole or nearly whole from previous performances. The actors played in companies that included both women and men, usually 10 or 12 actors in all, led by a player who functioned as actor-manager. Most companies worked on a partnership basis, though some of the less-experienced troupe members were probably salaried in the early years of participation.

The actors of the Italian *commedia dell'arte* toured widely, spending most of their time on the road, even though some companies were attached to the courts of the nobility. They played indoors or out, with or without scenery, under whatever physical conditions existed. They were versatile, highly respected professionals, who played all over Southern and Western Europe for two centuries. As such they had a very substantial influence on the development of the acting profession in the West. Their contribution was largely in the area of technique, though. There was little in Italian drama to sustain the

The comedies of the Roman playwright Terence were popular for centuries in Europe. (By Albrecht Dürer, late 15th century)

development of the kind of major theater that grew in other countries.

In opera, however, a different course of development occurred. Many of the artists and intellectuals of the Italian Renaissance were deeply impressed by the Greeks of the Golden Age. They sought to develop an Italian theater that could capture the style, depth, and total impact of the Greek theater, with its focus on music and vocal excellence. In pursuit of the Greek ideal, one group, the Camerata of Florence, commissioned a work, *Dafne*, by Ottavio Rinuccini, set to music by Jacopo Peri in 1594. This became the first opera. The opera proved enormously popular throughout Italy, and led to the works of Monteverde and scores of other early composers. A whole new theatrical-musical form developed, spreading far beyond Italy, with the musical aspects soon coming to dominate the theatrical. Those who perform in opera are primarily *musicians*, but musicians who are also actors. The line between opera and acted theater, always unclear, remains defined largely by the self-perception of those working on stage in these forms.

By the dawn of the 17th century, the acting profession was firmly established in many European countries. In Italy, England, France, and Spain, professional troupes enjoyed royal and noble sponsorship and noble protection. In England, before Elizabeth I, touring troupes could be—actually or in name only—under the sponsorship of any noble patron. But by 1572, national acting troupe sponsorships needed local licensing. Once licensed, however, actors were no longer likely to be jailed by local authorities as vagabonds—a constant hazard in earlier times, with or without noble sponsorship.

With protection and licensing, the theater was achieving more stability. In London, for example, permanent theaters were first built during the 1570's, providing a firmer physical basis for the development of the English theater. Licensing sometimes had the effect of concentrating theaters in one area. In England, the Stuart kings who followed Elizabeth tightened regulation of the theater; they restricted sponsorship of acting companies to members of the royal house and withdrew licensing of theaters outside the city. The result was to focus the development of the theater in London. London-based touring troupes remained, spending considerable time on the road in improvised theaters. But English actors spent more and more time working in permanent theaters after the turn of the century.

In many parts of Europe, theater companies organized on the Italian *commedia dell'arte* model, with actors as shareholders. That provided a measure of security to players in a notoriously uncertain profession. Many actors participated as co-owners, sharing both profits and risks, while others participated as *apprentices* and salaried troupe members. Among these were many working not as actors, but in other theater occupations, such as *costumers, musicians*, and *stagehands*.

Some actors even participated in ownership of the new permanent theaters that were beginning to be built. In 1598, Shakespeare and four other actors gained ownership shares in London's Globe Theater. This sparked a widespread move to partial actor-ownership of the English theaters, along with the already well established actor-management tradition of acting companies that existed throughout Europe.

European actors in the late 16th and early 17th centuries had extraordinary material with which to work on stage, for they presented new works produced by an astonishing generation of major dramatists. In England, they were working in Shakespeare's plays; in France, in the works of Molière; in Spain, in the dramas of Lope de Vega. The restrictions of the earlier church-dominated centuries began to diminish, and the actors of the period had great roles to create.

In France, the mid-17th century saw the beginning of royal subsidies for acting companies, and sharp changes in the legal status of actors. This was signaled by the royal decree of 1641, in which Louis XIII sought to make

the profession generally acceptable in French society. The Catholic Church in France continued to officially oppose the theater and the acting profession, but the powerful Cardinal Richelieu attended the theater and was influential in securing royal support for it.

In Italy, spectacles like this sea battle staged in Florence dominated the Renaissance theater. (Authors' archives, c. 1598)

Spain was the only major country in Europe in which religious plays had not been banned, and which established rigid censorship of the drama in 1608 and of the dance in 1615. But even there the theater enjoyed a period of tremendous vitality. The pay and status of Spanish actors improved markedly. They and other theater people formed a theater guild in 1641, which still exists.

During the previous centuries, from the Greeks to the Elizabethan Renaissance, the European theater had been largely a man's world. But the status of women in the theater was now changing sharply. Actresses had been active in Italy's *commedia dell'arte* and in the French theater, but few women had worked in the Spanish theater and none in England's Elizabethan theater. In Spain, women were legally permitted to work as actors by the decree of 1587. In England, male actors continued to play all the women's roles far into the 17th century.

The English Theater

In England, late in the 16th century, playwrights and players met to create an extraordinary Renaissance theater. This was the theater of the dramatists Thomas Kyd, Christopher Marlowe, Ben Jonson, and, above all, William Shakespeare. And it was the theater of the actors Richard Tarleton, Edward Alleyn, and especially Richard Burbage, who was the first to play such major roles as Lear, Hamlet, and Othello.

English actors in the 16th and 17th centuries worked in highly professional and closely regulated organizations. Acting was an apprenticeship occupation, with apprenticed boys playing children's and women's roles. The apprentices lived with their actor-masters during the years of apprenticeship, leaving them only on reaching maturity, and then sometimes continuing in the theater on their own.

Actors continued to have licensing problems well into the 17th century, but their status was slowly growing. Some became relatively well paid, as royal patronage grew, and as the theater established physical permanence and social acceptance on its own—at least until the Puritans' rise to power in 1642.

In that year, with the rise of Cromwell and the Puritans, the English theater came to an abrupt halt for a time. The new leaders of the country reasserted Christianity's traditional opposition to the theater and

the acting profession. Parliament closed the theaters in 1642, and kept them closed for as long as they held power, until the Restoration in 1660.

When English theaters reopened, it was with a new vitality—and a new look. Women suddenly appeared on the English stage in 1660. By the end of 1661, they were fully established in the English theater. Even so, some production companies introduced actresses with some hesitation, considering it prudent to "prepare" the audience. In a prologue to one such introduction, Thomas Jordan wrote:

Actors and variety performers played at country fairs and markets for many centuries. (By W.H. Pyne, from Picturesque Views of Rural Occupations in Early Nineteenth-Century England)

'Tis possible a vertuous women may
Abhor all sorts of looseness, and yet play;
Play on the stage, where all eyes are upon her,
Shall we count that a crime France counts an honour?

The restoration theater was in many respects an actor's theater and a *repertory* theater. That is, acting companies performed a certain collection of plays on a regular or rotating basis. For 150 years after the Restoration, English actors spent their careers in acting companies, developing specialties, playing to a considerable extent in ensemble, and working in a stable theatrical environment, even though government-theater relations were erratic.

By the end of that period, there were licensed theaters and companies all over Britain, in Ireland, and in the colonies, including the North American Colonies. England had a London-based theater, but there were many strong provincial companies, providing opportunities for substantial numbers of actors to practice their profession in companies enjoying theater structures, scenery, some rehearsal time—though repertory, then as now, afforded modest rehearsal times for most productions—and relatively predictable incomes.

Chinese actors like these Peking tragedians early developed a distinctive, stylized theater. (From Peoples of the World, *19th century)*

Actors' social status rose with stability and the decline of opposing church influences. Actors' pay became more a matter of salary than entrepreneurial (business ownership) sharing of risks and rewards, as investors and managers, rather than actors, formed companies and built theaters. In addition to salaries, the institution of the benefit performance for actors in a company began and lasted throughout the Restoration period. At least yearly, most companies would give a benefit performance, often at increased prices, and actors would share all revenue from that performance beyond house costs for the evening. In many instances, this substantially increased acting salaries for the year.

Acting continued to be an apprenticeship occupation, although several short-lived acting schools were attempted during the period. Some companies successfully ran in-company training activities for considerable times. Untrained actors normally joined companies as trainees, and spent years playing small roles and learning their trade by observing the work of experienced actors. Gradually they achieved more responsible character roles, and eventually settled into a fixed class of roles, which included both tragic and comic parts in the company's repertory.

In this period, actors were generally hired by the season, with leading actors contracted for longer terms. Late in the 18th century, however, some leading actors began to develop enough negotiating strength to be able to win considerably increased pay and shorter-term contracts. This signaled the beginning of the shift from the repertory system to the "star" system that would be the dominant course of development for actors in the Western theater from the beginning of the 19th century until today.

In the mid-18th century, a new way of acting began to take shape, which also was to become dominant in modern times. It was the mode of *realism*—the use of more natural, lifelike patterns of speech and movement on stage—strongly identified with the great actors

Throughout history, actors have been supported by a hard-working stage crew; here the Drury Lane Theatre is being altered between engagements. (New York Public Library, Theater Collection)

David Garrick and Charles Macklin. Before their time, acting had been performed in what was thought to be the Classic Greek and Roman mode of delivery, with actors tending to declaim long, singing, sonorous lines. In this, the theater had been much like opera, which continued, as it had begun, in the Classic mode. In a very real sense, the English theater of the late 18th century was a theater beginning to be the modern European theater in style, structure, and financial arrangements; and the profession of acting paralleled that development.

Acting on the Continent

The actors of France, Germany, and elsewhere on the Continent experienced a course of development similar to that of their English counterparts of the 16th, 17th, and 18th centuries. There were important differences between countries regarding the development of their national theaters, but for working actors the similarities far outweighed the differences.

In France, the simultaneous impact of the Italian *commedia dell'arte* companies and the development of the neoclassical movement in drama during the first half of the 16th century early created the conditions within which French Renaissance acting could begin. By 1539, an early dramatic organization, the *Confrérie de la Passion*, had been granted sole rights to theater production in Paris. By mid-century it was presenting plays at the first public theater in France, the Hôtel de Bourgogne. By 1581, several early ballets had been produced, foreshadowing the later development of the ballet.

Religious civil wars virtually stopped the development of the French theater for a time at the end of the 16th century. But during the early 17th century, the first touring acting companies working in Paris performed at the Hôtel de Bourgogne. Their most popular offerings were comedies called *farces*. In this period, actors working in the French touring companies were usually shareholders, and women actors were included as members of the companies. Neither companies nor individual actors were state supported. The theater was purely private and commercial, with the actors' trade carrying much of the scandalous reputation attached to it by the Christian church of the Middle Ages.

By the 1630's, dramatists and actors were producing some of the great plays of the French theater, and two permanent troupes had settled in Paris. Both soon received royal financial support and approval. Such financial support served to help stabilize the new French theater, while the approval served to sharply change the social status of those in the theater professions. Actors such as the great tragic actor Montdory were then beginning to appear in the works of such playwrights as Pierre Corneille and Jean de Mairet, and later in the century in the works of Jean Racine and Molière.

In 1680, the Comédie Française was formed by royal decree, a combination of two previous companies. It was the first modern European national theater, that is, a theater company sponsored by the national government.

Like the other companies, it was a sharing company, with some actors on salary and some sharing risks and profits. Unlike many other companies, however, those actors holding shares in the Comédie Française—the only government-authorized drama company in Paris—signed 20-year contracts, in essence making their careers with that company. As in all French companies, actors in this period played in repertory. Given the company's unique position, it is not surprising that when the Royal Dramatic School was formed in 1786, it was attached to the Comédie Française. Before that time, actors started in minor roles, as *understudies*, and gradually developed into more substantial roles, as was true in England.

The French Revolution ended the system of royal patronage, and for a time halted the main course of development of the French theater. But not for long, as Napoléon soon reinstated government licensing and subsidies for theaters. After Napoléon, French theater and French actors began to move into the modern period.

Actors in Italy and Spain worked under conditions very similar to those of France and England in the 16th, 17th, and 18th centuries. In Spain, strict censorship was a special problem, but social position less so than in England and France. In Italy, national interest turned toward the opera as the main national theater form, after the early impact of the Italian Renaissance theater on all of Europe.

In the rest of Europe, actors had little chance to develop their craft until late in the 18th century, for it was only then that the German states, Austria-Hungary, Russia, Scandinavia, and the Low Countries began to develop a modern theater. In the many German-speaking states, including Austria-Hungary, the last quarter of the 18th century brought establishment of scores of subsidized national theaters and many other city-sponsored theaters, all with resident acting companies. In a very short time, this created a major new audience for German-speaking actors and dramatists. The major acting form was the realistic Hamburg style developed by the great actor-manager Friedrich Schröder, whose Hamburg National Theater company was the leading company of the German-speaking theater until the end of the 18th century. However, the tightly disciplined ensemble style of Johann Wolfgang von Goethe's Weimar Theater supplied a contrasting style,which was to be of considerable importance in the development of German acting styles and the German theater.

The Russian theater, which was later to develop acting styles widely used in the modern theater, was in its early period patterned after the French theater. It was state supported, strictly regulated, and censored. The Russian national theater was established in 1756, and a state-sponsored acting school in 1779. The Russian theater would move onto the general European stage only late in the 19th century, with the development of the modern theater.

The Modern Western Theater

During the early part of the 19th century, European and American actors continued to work mainly in repertory companies. The number of both state-supported and private theater companies rose rapidly. In England, the United States, the German states, France, and later in Russia, large new theater-going audiences formed, with important long-range results for the acting profession. New audiences and more public and private support meant more opportunities; as a result, many more actors came into the profession. In England, for example, a huge population increase and substantial new mass interest in the theater caused the expansion of existing licensed theaters. Scores of new houses opened in London and throughout the British Isles during the first half of the 19th century. And starting in 1843 any licensed theater was able to produce any kind of work. In France, the few authorized Parisian companies operating at the beginning of the 19th century had become 28 by 1855. In the German states, there were 65 state-supported theaters by 1842, whose actors were state employees. In the new United States, the few provincial companies of Colonial days had become well over 30 permanent companies and many smaller touring companies by mid-century.

The uncertain began to give way to the "sure thing." The long-run play featuring an established star began to replace repertory. Leading players began to successfully demand contracts limited to a season, the run of a play, or even a group of performances—all at far higher rates of pay than leading players in repertory had received. During the 18th century, sharing companies had, in most instances, become salaried companies, with managers and investors reaping whatever profits were to be gained from theatrical performances; now some of the actors began to take a significant share once again. The only major exception was the Comédie Française, which continued to be a sharing company. Only where all or most actors were state employees were actors prevented from reaping new financial benefits from the new audience for the theater.

By the late 19th century, actors were working in a theater that was in many significant respects much like the live theater of the late 20th century. Realism in speech, action, stage business, costumes, and sets was the dominant mode of stage presentation. Actors played mainly as salaried performers for the run of the play, rather than in repertory, and most plays were built around stars.

By then, the advent of the railroad networks covering Europe and North America had begun to reverse the trend toward many permanent companies and houses, as it had become possible to put a whole show, complete with sets and costumes—and, most important, complete with star or stars—on tour. Since it was the stars the public wanted, the permanent local companies began to disappear, being replaced by touring companies. Plays became far more elaborate and expensive to mount.

This was the period of the actor-manager-entrepreneur, such as the great Henry Irving, a key force in the English theater during the late 19th century; and of Konstantin Stanislavsky's Moscow Art Theater, which had a profound influence on acting styles throughout the world during the 20th century.

This was also the period in which the apprenticeship training methods of the English and American theaters began to change somewhat. In 1884, the school that would become the American Academy of Dramatic Art was founded, foreshadowing a time when thousands of young American actors would receive formal training every year, before entering the professional world of acting. In 1904, the school that would become the Royal Academy of Dramatic Art (RADA) was founded in England.

Although the acting profession widened considerably during the 19th century, it narrowed toward the end of that century. As regional companies closed, the permanent theater companies—and therefore the acting profession—became more and more concentrated in a few major cities, especially New York, London, and Paris. Unless they were fortunate enough to become part of a long run in a major city, actors once more—as in the old days—became creatures of the "circuit," traveling with one of the many touring companies. Not until the development of the regional and repertory theater movements in the late 20th century were actors again able to pursue their careers outside the major cities in which the profession was concentrated. Even then, major opportunities to play leading roles on stage were still clustered in a few theater centers.

In the 20th century, new technologies opened up entirely new opportunities for actors, and the profession expanded enormously. Movies, radio, and television gave actors whole new kinds of careers that had never before been possible. By the late part of the 20th century, a professional actor could in any given year work on stage, as a disembodied voice on radio, and on screen in movies or television. Most professional actors belonged to one or more unions and had some professional training before seeking full-time work. Most actors worked production by production, whether that production was a stage play, a single television or radio commercial, or a long-running television series. Some worked in repertory, among them the regional theater players in the United States, Canada, and Great Britain.

The star system, which had started late in the 18th century, was even more fully the dominant mode. Some stars achieved great economic success, especially in movies and television, and undertook the classic actor-manager-entrepreneur roles so characteristic of late-19th century theater. In the American film industry, for example, such actors as Charles Chaplin and Mary Pickford very early undertook entrepreneurial roles by forming their own production company. Even when the major Hollywood studios were dominant, such actors as Katharine Hepburn were active in the acquisition and sale of film properties. And from the 1950's on, after the breakdown of the major studio system, such film stars as Burt Lancaster often formed their own production companies. The practice also was adopted by leading players in American television, with such stars as Lucille Ball and Mary Tyler Moore developing their own production companies. The main mode of theater presentation in all forms continued to be realism. The social status of actors throughout the world was better than it had been at any time since the Greek Golden Age. In some ways it was even better than it had been 2,500 years earlier, for the actor Ronald Reagan had even been elected president of the United States.

The new forms in which actors have worked in the 20th century are truly worldwide forms, and have served to spread Western concepts of drama and realism to most countries. Elements of the Western theater had entered Asian drama as early as the 17th and 18th centuries. They were first introduced by Western imperial occupiers and later adopted by choice into the national theaters of

The pose of this heroine, Mary Anderson, would be instantly recognizable to any 19th-century melodrama audience. (By Napoleon Sarony, 1833, Library of Congress)

the rest of the world. Movies and television programs in the late 20th century are made in the Western style throughout the Third World. Major national film centers exist in India and Japan, and Hong Kong produces films in several languages, aimed at audiences all over South and East Asia. All forms of the modern Western theater are to be found in the East and throughout the Third World. Even in nonfundamentalist Islamic countries, the Islamic prohibitions that long stifled the development of the theater have to some extent given way, and the acting profession has emerged in such countries as Egypt and Turkey.

But Asian actors developed their work in contexts rather different from those of the West. The Eastern and Western theaters did have strong ties for thousands of years—at least through the Byzantine period—and cross-cultural influences have yet to be fully explored. The differences, however, are strong enough to warrant some separate consideration of actors in the East and West.

Actors in India

The great early theater of Asia was that of the Indian subcontinent. Like the Greek theater of the West, it had enormous impact on all that followed in the area it influenced. Unlike the Greek theater, however, it experienced a far less broken course of development. As a result, continuous and intertwined performing and dramatic traditions grew during a period lasting well over 1,200 years, from before the beginning of the Christian era in the West to the period of Moslem dominance in the East. This tradition survived and developed in Southeast Asia through to modern times, and had a profound influence upon the theaters of East Asia, now the Chinese, Japanese, and Korean theaters. Indian civilization is old—as old, or very nearly so, as the civilizations of Mesopotamia, Egypt, and China. And Indian theater is old, probably older than that of Greece, though its major dramatic works came some hundreds of years after those of the Greek Golden Age.

Some 2000 years B.C., Indo-Aryan invaders from the north began to conquer the main states of the Indian subcontinent. These were the same people who, in Europe, were known as Indo-Europeans, and who also peopled Persia (now Iran). Their language was Sanskrit, and in that language they developed one of the world's great early literatures. The *Rigveda*, their earliest-known religious literary work, dates from about 1400 B.C. The *Ramayana* (Saga of Rama) and the *Mahabharata* (Great War of the Bharata) are dated in finished form somewhat later, but are epics of extraordinary length, thought to have been developed over a period of centuries, starting as early as 1500 B.C. These epics provided a great deal of material from which Indian and other South Asian drama were to be derived for well over 2,000 years. The *Arthra Sastra* (Doctrine of Prosperity), an extended set of comments on Indian life and society, reaches back in part to the fourth century B.C.

We are unable to date the start of the acting profession in India as we can in Greece, for here no Thespis steps out upon the world stage at an identifiable time and place. Integrated stage works requiring actors, dancers, musicians, and costumers were written as early as 100 A.D., and some sources claim that dramatic works were being written hundreds of years earlier. The appearance of the *Natya Sastra* (The Science of Dramaturgy) no later than 200 A.D., and possibly as early as 200 B.C., argues strongly for the earlier dates; this very long and detailed examination of every aspect of classical Sanskrit theater was the kind of work that could only have been produced after development of a long theater tradition. The *Natya Sastra* is a manual intended for use by those in highly formalized theater, carrying instructions covering every aspect of acting, dance, music, makeup, and costuming.

All those elements existed in the Sanskrit theater, side by side and intertwined—and they continued to exist all during the long development of Asian theater. Asian performers work in a theater joining all the elements of performance, even though Asian national theaters and genres within national theaters may differ. In this respect all Asian theater is sharply different from the theater that evolved in the West. Western stage performers, as distinct from circus, carnival, and puppet troupes, perform in somewhat compartmentalized areas of the performing arts, such as drama, opera, or ballet.

Some hundreds of Sanskrit dramas were written and

performed, with the golden age of Indian drama variously placed between 100 A.D. and 800 A.D. The peak of the golden age is generally thought to be in the fifth century, with the work of the great poet-dramatist Kalidasa, especially his master work, *Shakuntala*. Another peak was reached in the seventh century A.D., in the work of the poet-dramatist-king, Harsha, who ruled much of India and Southeast Asia.

Sanskrit drama was the drama of the ruling elites, performed by players trained in and attached to the courts of the nobility. According to the *Natya Sastra*, troupes of performers consisted of a *master actor*, or *troupe leader*, a *clown, actor-dancers, musicians,* and a body of *costumers* and *stagecraft technicians*. They included women, sometimes playing male roles, and men, sometimes playing women's roles. Only during the period of Moslem domination were women forced off the Indian stage, to reappear only in modern times. The troupes, though attached to courts, are also believed to have traveled, moving from court to court.

Even though Sanskrit drama players were some of the great artists of their time, their social status was very low, like that of other Indian performers. They worked in a highly structured society, which had begun the process of stratification as early as 600 B.C., and their status was that of people on the fringes of society.

Sanskrit was the universal language of Indian literature. Its poetry and drama were matters of high art, with performers and players joining in the creation of theatrical experience. This was not the theater of the great mass of the Indian population, however, for by about the beginning of the Christian era in the West, Sanskrit was no longer in general use for everyday conversation. (In this it is like Latin in late medieval Europe.) Even the ruling elites of the many Indian states used local dialects during the golden age of the Sanskrit drama.

As is still true in Asian theater, traveling troupes of players worked in the many dialects of the Indian subcontinent. These artists, like the traveling troupes of

Etruria and Rome, moved constantly in the towns and countryside, playing at festivals for very little pay, enjoying very little social status, and pursuing their craft. Their work continued, surviving the impact of Islam, and provided a link between the golden age of Indian drama and the theater of today, much as the art of the traveling players and minstrels of Europe survived the end of Rome, and informed the theater of the Renaissance.

From its known beginnings, Indian theater has been highly stylized, its performers trained in formal, abstract, and completely categorized modes of expression, in which realistic expression had no place. With the impact of Western theater, first as brought by the British occupiers and later with the development of a worldwide film industry, Indian mass audiences in the 20th century have turned decisively toward Western forms, performed by actors who characteristically infuse their work with the stylized approaches of the Indian past. Although many touring folk troupes continue to work in traditional styles, the mass media, as in the West, has become increasingly dominant. The hodgepodge that often results may properly be viewed as only a transitional form.

The classic Indian theater greatly influenced the developing theater of Southeast Asia, and continues to influence live theater there in the 20th century, even while the mass media turn audiences more and more toward Western forms. During the Indian theater's Golden Age, Indian epic literature (though not the Indian dramatic forms as detailed in the *Natya Sastra*) provided the material from which much of the improvisational dramatic theater of Southeast Asia was developed. On Java, Sunda, and especially on Bali—which was the only island to maintain its Hindu culture and withstand Islam—Indian literature and native drama developed in the Indian tradition provided continuity. In 20th-century Indonesia, hundreds and perhaps thousands of theater troupes continue to play in over a score of traditional forms.

The traditional form of troupe organization continues to be that of ownership by an actor-manager-entrepreneur, with salaried players. Troupes continue to present work that is based upon a preset story line, but that, in its details, is largely improvisational. Each performance is therefore similar in line but different in language and, to some extent, in stage business. And, as was and is true of the Indian theater, the theater of Southeast Asia continues to be wholly integrated, with artists acting, dancing, singing, often playing instruments, and practicing many of the variety arts, such as juggling, rope walking, acrobatics, and magic.

Actors in China

Although India was the home of the great early Asian theater, it is in Chinese culture and society that we find the longest uninterrupted development of a classic theater, a theater that has for over a thousand years formally trained actors and other theater people in a set of extraordinarily high-level performing traditions. Once again, we see in China no Thespis striding upon the Asian stage. Instead, we see 3,000 years of performing arts development, starting with the practice of such popular arts as juggling, mime, dance, music, athletics, and tightrope walking, performed at the courts of the Chinese emperors as early as 1000 to 800 B.C. By the time of the Han emperors, the early theatrical arts were collectively called the "hundred plays."

But it was not until the sixth century A.D. that the classic Chinese theater began to emerge, by then influenced considerably by the Indian theater. Like that theater, it integrated all elements, including acting, dancing, music, and pantomime, and tended toward highly formalized and stylized forms of presentation. In 714 A.D., the T'ang Emperor Hsüan Tsung started the first national Chinese school for the performing arts, called the "School of the Pear Garden." For Chinese actors, this event symbolizes the beginning of the actor's art in China. They are therefore called "students of the Pear Garden."

The School of the Pear Garden was large, being estimated as offering full-time training to a body of over 1,000 actors, singers, and dancers. Other schools were formed as well, establishing a tradition of professional training in the theater arts that was to continue until modern times. The artists trained in the emperor's schools were at first destined only for performance in the emperor's court. Some were not so much trained for performance as to have performing arts skills, in addition to being *prostitutes*, variously called *concubines* and *courtesans*, in the emperor's court. But the system and tradition of training started then was to supply trained theater people to professional troupes all over China. During the 10th through 12th centuries, professional performers played not only in the emperor's court, but in theater buildings and as traveling troupes all over China.

Although the beginnings of Chinese literature go back to at least 1500 B.C. and although Chinese theater and artistic performances are traceable back at least as far, it was the late 13th century A.D. that saw the main joining of dramatist and player in China. During the 11th and 12th centuries, writers had begun to create sustained works for the stage, writing in folk forms and in the vernacular (the commonly spoken language) for the acting companies that were beginning to tour widely in China, as they would for a thousand years. But writing for the theater was looked upon as a very minor art by Chinese writers, who were by then working in philosophy, history, language, the sciences, and poetry.

The Mongol invasion created the conditions within which those perceptions changed. The Mongols, who held China from 1279 to 1368, the period of the Yüan dynasty, abolished the civil service examinations and many of the positions that had provided employment for most educated people. Many of these unemployed scholars took a new interest in the folk forms, especially in writing for the theater. The resulting body of work, performed by already well-established and highly skilled Chinese theater companies, was China's equivalent of the Renaissance theater of the West. Such 13th-century works as the best-known play of the period, Wang Shih-fu's *Romance of the West Chamber*, and Li Ch'ien'fu's *The Story of the Chalk Circle* (later adapted in the West by Bertolt Brecht into *The Caucasion Chalk Circle*), were created by the dramatists of the northern school, centered in Peking. Toward the middle of the 14th century, a body of dramatists appeared in the south, as well, centered in Hangchow. Keo Ming's *Lute Song* is the best-known work of the southern school.

North and south, Chinese actors worked in a theater characterized by small, enclosed theater structures, almost bare stages, and rather elaborate costumes; drama was presented essentially as musical theater, in which speech, songs, music, and dance were fully integrated. Although working in folk forms and in the vernacular, Chinese actors worked in fixed and abstracted modes of expression on stage. They developed no equivalent of the realistic style of presentation until the impact of Western theater was felt much later in Chinese history. Chinese drama continued to develop as musical theater after the Golden Age of the Yüan dynasty. The southern school became dominant by the 16th century, and even more musically oriented in succeeding centuries. By the mid-19th century, it had declined, giving way to the Peking Opera, from then until 1949 the dominant theater form in China.

The Peking Opera is essentially a musically oriented variety theater, featuring many actors, singers, dancers, and other variety performers, such as acrobats and jugglers, all accompanied by and integrated with a group of musicians, who are visible and very much part of the stage proceedings. Excerpts from plays written in earlier periods are performed, as well as more contemporary skits and acts. Actors work on stages and in costumes very much like those of earlier centuries, adhering to a body of performance conventions hundreds of years old.

Women were barred from the Chinese stage from the mid-19th century until the victory of Sun Yat-Sen, who established the Chinese Republic of 1911; men played all the women's roles during that period. Both women and men performing in the Chinese theater suffered from very low status in Chinese society for most of the 2,000 years of recorded Chinese theater history. This was not a matter of religious opposition, as in the Christian and Moslem worlds. To some extent, it was a question of the popular identification of women actors with the performance-trained prostitutes of the imperial courts; it may also have been that, in a very stable, family-oriented society, travelers were given low status.

With the invasion, or "opening up," of China by the Western nations in the mid-19th century, the Chinese theater, like all China, entered a period of considerable change. The development of a substantial number of regional variations on the Peking Opera accelerated, and some Western elements entered traditional styles in a few areas. After the revolution of 1911, Western plays were presented in China, classics were adapted from the Chinese theater into Western or "spoken" styles, and some Chinese playwrights began to create spoken plays. Chinese theater companies, however, continued to operate much as they had before. Companies were led by actor-manager-entrepreneurs. Performers and other company members worked for salaries by the season, mostly in touring companies.

After the founding of the Communist People's Republic of China in 1949, the Chinese theater became a state theater, and dramatists turned toward political themes and more toward spoken than musical theater. Actors, however, continue to work in a theater that stresses a high degree of training, presents its work in traditional modes, and integrates all theater elements in the long and unbroken performance traditions of the Chinese theater.

Actors in Japan

The integration of all the elements of theater into each performance is a major characteristic of East Asian theater. That is a main feature of the Korean theater, for example, so deeply influenced by Chinese theater and Chinese acting modes, and of those areas of Southeast Asia influenced by Chinese culture. It is true of Japanese theater, as well, although Japanese theater and its performers embarked upon a distinctly Japanese course of development in the 11th and 12th centuries. They built a major theater form and body of work starting in the 14th century, called the *Noh* theater.

Buddhism came to Japan near the beginning of the seventh century A.D., and with it an opening to the art forms of China, India, and Korea. During the next three centuries, a substantial body of dancers, musicians, mimes, and acrobats were trained and subsidized by the imperial court. These performers played in a number of basically dance-drama forms, the most important of which were *bugaku*, describing traditional court dances; *saragaku-no* (monkey music), a comedy-variety music form, which is a combination of several national forms transplanted to Japan; and *dengaku-no*, a country festival dance form.

During the 12th century, both *saragaku-no* and *dengaku-no* were transformed into religious teaching forms, a development paralleling that of the Western medieval morality plays of the same period. *Saragaku-no* was used by the Buddhist clergy and *dengaku-no* by the Shinto clergy. In Europe, the medieval morality plays were in the main played by amateurs, with the Renaissance theater developing as a mostly secular form. In Japan, development was quite different. The professional players of the *saragaku-no* and *dengaku-no* were soon organized in professional companies attached to and subsidized by temples and shrines. These were players in a theatrical tradition, which by the 14th century went back some hundreds of years. The *dengaku-no* and *saragaku-no* players formed their first guilds during the 12th century.

In 1192, Japan entered into the period of the *shoguns* (military rulers), which was to last until the return of the emperor to the throne in 1868. This was the long period of feudal military domination, during which Japan was governed by a succession of families with control of military power. The Noh theater developed with the sponsorship and support of the Ashikaga family shogunate, which ruled during most of the 14th through 16th centuries. In 1374, the great *saragaku-no* player, Kannami Kiyotsugu, and his young son, Zeami Motokiyo, were attached to the court of the shogunate of Yoshimitsu Ashikaga. Kannami created what was essentially a performers' theater, merging *saragaku-no*, Zen Buddhism, and other popular music-dance forms into a new court form, which was to be the main aristocratic Japanese theatrical form until the 20th century. Zeami, who was both player and writer, further developed the form. He wrote over a hundred plays that are still part of the Noh repertory, and developed and wrote basic aesthetic and practical works on the new form, which became guides followed by all future Noh performers.

The Noh theater is primarily a dance-drama theater, with music always present. Every element of performance is prescribed; every movement and sound, however minor, is performed traditionally, with no variance from established practice. In essence, each play is a ritual dance set to music.

Noh performers from the first all have been male. They work on stage in masks, in rather elaborate traditional costumes, without scenery, and with few props other than fans, which are used to suggest the passage of events. Noh performers are trained from very early in life to convey the values of Zen Buddhism within the context of the Noh stage in the traditional forms. Often they are members of families who have been performing in the Noh theater for many generations. On stage with them, playing during intermissions, and sometimes taking minor roles in Noh performances, are the players of the kyōgen theater, who perform comic pieces without music. Theirs is essentially a farce theater, functioning to provide counterpoint for the Noh plays. After the end of the shogunate, the Noh theater lost its financial source. However, within a few years, the emperor had supplied some support, as had other segments of society. Noh survives in modern Japan as a major traditional theater form.

The other major form within which Japanese actors worked was the *Kabuki* theater. (Puppetry, also a major theater form in Japan, is discussed in a separate article on *puppeteers*.) Unlike the Noh theater, the Kabuki theater was a popular and secular theater, drawing upon several other contemporary forms in the course of developing its own identity. From the puppet theater, which developed side by side with it starting in the early 17th century, it took many of the plays in its repertoire, while it drew many of its acting forms and stage practices from the Noh theater.

Kabuki developed as a secular dance theater, as dancers attached to Buddhist and Shinto shrines began to develop popular performances and a secular audience. One of the earliest Kabuki performers we know of was Okuni, a woman dancer of Kyoto. In 1603, with other women and a few men, she played to popular audiences very successfully—so successfully that she attracted large crowds and many competitors. However, in 1629, the shogunate banned women from the Kabuki stage as offensive to public morals. They were not to return to that stage until after the end of the shogunate in 1868, almost two and one-half centuries later.

Women were succeeded by boys and young men. But these performers were likewise banned in 1652 by the shogunate as offensive to public morals. They were succeeded by men, who were the only players on the Kabuki stage for two centuries. These men took considerable care to remove sexual elements from their performances, from the first adopting the convention of head shaving, which continues even today. In later centuries, the banning of women from the Kabuki stage led to the development of the *onnagata* (female impersonator), a role that often became central in Kabuki drama. Even with the end of that ban after 1868, the Kabuki theater remained totally male, although the modern Japanese theater is fully open to men and women actors.

In Kabuki theater, as in Noh theater, dance is predominant. But Kabuki players worked far more with a changing body of plays in a theater that lived and developed, rather than fixing itself firmly in its early forms. The early Kabuki theater was almost entirely dance-oriented, but by the end of the 17th century, playwrights who wrote for both the Kabuki and puppet theaters were producing a considerable body of work. The best known of these playwrights was Chikamatsu Monzaemon, who wrote 100 to 150 plays for the puppet and Kabuki theaters, his puppet theater plays also later appearing in the Kabuki repertory. New works continued to be written for the Kabuki theater until the mid-18th century, often by playwrights attached to the Kabuki companies. These were not fully scripted, in the modern Western style, but resembled some of the European *commedia dell'arte* works, being partly scripted in scenes and acts, and to some extent developed by the players as they worked on stage.

Kabuki players worked on stage without masks, though often in heavy makeup. They used rather elaborate costumes, often based on traditional attire; fans, as on the Noh stage, but with many other props as well; considerable scenery; and, after the first quarter of the 17th century, an increasingly complex body of stage machinery that was fully as elaborate as that used in the West.

Like so much of South and East Asian theater, the Kabuki theater is highly stylized, and players usually undergo very long and intensive training. In Kabuki, this is apprenticeship training, with young children starting in the theater in children's roles, and moving on into mature roles in the course of careers spanning many decades.

Although the Kabuki and Noh theaters continue in modern Japan, the Western theater began to be introduced after 1868, with increasing impact on Japanese theater and performers in the 20th century. Western dramas, acting styles, and stagecraft all had been introduced by the first decade of the century. Then, as the worldwide film industry began to grow, Japanese actors moved en masse into what quickly became a very large Japanese film industry. In the mid-20th century, when television grew into a second worldwide screen industry, audiences created massive opportunities for Japanese players. Today, Japanese actors, like actors all over the world, can work in traditional as well as modern forms, in work destined for stage or screen, within a context of increasing celebrity for some and considerable respect for all.

For related occupations in this volume, *Performers and Players*, see the following:
  Dancers
  Directors
  Musicians
  Puppeteers
  Variety Performers

For related occupations in other volumes of the series, see the following:
in *Communicators*:
  Authors
in *Leaders and Lawyers*:
  Political Leaders
in *Restaurateurs and Innkeepers* (forthcoming):
  Prostitutes
in *Scholars and Priests*:
  Priests
  Scholars
  Teachers

Athletes

Professionalism in modern sport is sometimes described as having evolved from the sacred to the profane. Most ancient games—what we would now call *sports*—were designed as rituals to honor, entreat, or thank the gods. People often sought the grace of their gods in peacetime, and their direct intervention and assistance in wartime; such entreaties formed an important part of ancient life. Athletes in early history, then, were seen as mediums in human communication with the supernatural, devoted to their ritualistic roles. Training and contests were also often militaristic, so athletes were considered to be prototypes of patriotism. In ancient times, war was considered a religious undertaking in which nations often battled to uphold the sanctity of their gods.

The earliest athletes, then, were not *professionals* in the sense of people earning a livelihood through participation in play, nor were they *amateurs*, in the sense of people playing sheerly for fun. They were, rather, citizens performing religious rites to please the gods, or *soldiers* seeking the additional benefits of better physical conditioning and learning styles of combat—two essential ingredients in enforcing the will of the gods.

In Mesopotamia—the flat, fertile land lying between the great Tigris and Euphrates rivers in what is now modern Iraq—constant warfare between cities led inevitably to combat-style sports and games, but for all the sporting activity in Mesopotamia, there is no evidence of anything like professional athletes, apart from soldiers. Soldiers served their city-state by performing the divine will at war, while appeasing the gods with their military-athletic displays at special assemblies. Being athletic was a requirement for being a soldier. All Persian soldiers, for instance, were expected to be expert in physical events and athletics, and festivals were often arranged for the purpose of displaying their prowess.

In ancient Egypt, also, military training was the scene of athletic performance and contest. Wrestling, archery, and combat sports were commonly used toward this end by 2000 B.C. Great teams of *wrestlers* were depicted on the walls of the tomb of Beni-Hasan of the Twelfth Dynasty. These groups were probably not professional, but the wealthy classes clearly enjoyed watching them perform. Another popular form of athletic entertainment for upper-class spectators was acrobatic shows, performed primarily by women. Professional *acrobats* were active at this time, and were some of the earliest athletes to be paid for their displays of talent and skill. Bands of professional acrobats entertained the wealthy on special occasions, and playing with balls became an important feature of their show. A sort of team play may even have evolved in this type of ball-playing. While working-class people apparently participated in athletic games, although not as professionals, the upper classes generally confined their activities to board games.

The first great period of Egyptian history—from about 2700 to 2200 B.C.—is significant in that it clearly marks the evolution of the god-king concept. The great pharaohs of the age, such as Khufu and Khaf-Re, sat apart from human aspirations, including athletic displays, showing no active or passive interest in sports or physical contests. By around 1550 to 1375 B.C., however, the pharaoh had a new role to fulfill, that of a physically strong and energetic conqueror of the frontier. This ushered in a new age in which archery, wrestling, running, and the like were vigorously participated in not only by the common people and the nobility, but also by the pharaoh himself, to whom was attributed superhuman athletic feats. Thutmose III is said to have driven an arrow nearly nine inches out of the back of a two-inch-thick copper target. Amenhotep II, the most athletic of them all, is credited with having driven an arrow clear through a three-inch-thick copper target. In addition, he was an expert *equestrian* (horse-rider) and *rower*, and was hailed as the fastest *runner* alive. Physical accomplishment was still, however, an offering to the gods, even when accomplished by the pharaoh, who was considered a god himself.

Soldiers also followed the pharaoh's lead in pursuing sports, as part of their military training. If nothing else, the better warriors stood to gain the most when it was time to divide up the spoils of a defeated foe. There is little evidence that the general population had much to do with sports at all, although this may not be significant, because ancient records focus heavily on the affairs of the nobility. What sport did exist in this period was primarily individual, noncompetitive, and participatory. Later, as Egyptian civilization declined, sports became more spectator- and-contest oriented, although the athletes themselves continued to be almost exclusively members of the nobility and military classes.

The Minoan and Mycenaean civilizations of the Aegean Sea did not contribute significantly to the further development of professionalism in sport. Perhaps their greatest contribution in this respect was in their strong inclination toward spectator sports, most notably *taureador* (bull-grappling) sports. (The modern *toreador* in bullfighting takes his name from this.) As they were developed in Crete in the Minoan period (from around 3000 to 1550 B.C.), taureador sports were largely acrobatic, performed by athletes of considerable skill. Women filled this role as well as men, and may have formed a distinct professional class. The events were originally ceremonial and religious, although we know little of their particular significance.

In the Minoan period and in the Mycenaean Age that followed, from about 1550 to 1100 B.C., wrestling and running drew crowds of both men and women, but only boxing rivaled bull-grappling sports in popularity. These boxing events were not the paired boxing matches that we are accustomed to, which became common in Greece soon after. Instead, they appear to have been group affairs in which large numbers of *boxers* fought in patterns geared particularly toward pleasing the spectators. The boxers were part of professional companies that journeyed throughout the land. While Mesopotamian and Egyptian athletes were generally of high social ranking (except for acrobats, who were drawn from the lower classes), Greek boxers were slaves, captives, or mercenaries (people working purely for pay). In general, professional athletes in pre-Hellenic Greece seem to have been of low social ranking and of either sex, while military athletes were almost exclusively males of high social ranking, either by birth or through acquired military status.

Aristocratic and military sports were popular in ancient China and Japan, and professional groups of *wrestlers* attracted large followings throughout India. Little is known of ancient Indian athletes, but we do know that professional wrestlers there trained from early childhood to attain bulk, and presumably strength, to perform well in their contests. Some form of *football* was popular in China by 600 B.C., as were wrestling and the martial arts. *Jiu-jitzu* was first developed there, but was perfected in Japan by the exclusive military caste—the Samurai. Sports in East Asia seem to have been similar to those in the Western world in being basically aristocratic, generally related to some sort of military training or fighting technique, and seldom either professional- or spectator-oriented.

In the period before the great Greek and Roman eras, then, there seem to have been very few professional athletes, and no professional athletic guilds or organizations. The few professionals were of low social class and performed primarily for an upper-class audience. In contrast, military athletes were highly regarded for the patriotic and therefore religious missions they undertook. While sports in their hands were essentially ritualistic and unspecialized, we see in them the beginnings of sporting competition and athletic training. Spectator sports—a prerequisite for the establishment of professional athleticism—tended to develop where and when there was sufficient wealth to create a leisure class. These spectator events tended to be dramatic and sensational, and the professional athletes who performed in them appear to have been much more *performers* or *entertainers* than players.

Greek Athletes

Ancient Greece is legendary as the birthplace of the sporting spirit, of play for the sake of play—in other words, amateurism. Historically, it is often difficult to tell where professionalism had made inroads into traditionally amateur events. Certainly ancient Greek games were often designed specifically to discourage mercenaries from competing in "pure"—that is, amateur—athletic contests. The prize in these early games was a simple laurel wreath, not riches. The amateurism of the Hellenic world, however, was very different from that of the earlier Egyptian and Minoan-Mycenaean cultures.

Greek sport before the Age of Homer served many purposes. Amateur sport had religious use in its ceremonial and ritualistic forms, military use in its training programs, and political use in its display of the supremacy of the ruling class. But professional sport had run quite a different course. It is difficult to find any religious significance to public bull-grappling or boxing. Professional athletes were not soldiers, nor did they perform military exercises or engage in training that would make them fit warriors. To the contrary, many trained specifically to entertain an audience, thereby benefiting from gate receipts. Because of the casual nature of these sports, and because the athletes—often slaves and women—had no official standing in their governments or in the military, they could hardly have served any political purpose.

The Age of Homer is well known for its love of sport, as related in Homer's epic poems, the *Iliad* and the *Odyssey*. Although written between the eighth and ninth centuries B.C., they speak about the earliest days of

For the Greeks, athletes like this disc thrower partook of more beauty than blood. (From Men: A Pictorial Archive From Nineteenth-Century Sources, *by Jim Harter, Dover, 1980)*

Hellenic Greece, the 11th and 12th centuries B.C. The *Iliad* tells us that the early Achaean Greek warriors were all athletes. Sports in the form of funeral games were taken up in strict amateur fashion, as a ceremonial form of play. In the *Odyssey*, Odysseus participates in the afterdinner games of the Greeks, including footracing, wrestling, and boxing.

Obviously, the sports of this age were without passive audiences or substantial rewards. They were engaged in for enjoyment in the purest sense of the word *amateur*. In fact, the meaning of the word *athlete* then was similar to modern understanding of the word *amateur*. The athletes of the Homeric Age were even more purely amateurs than those of the modern age. They, too, played for fun and honor, but—unlike modern amateurs—the Homeric athletes did not perform with thoughts of one day becoming highly paid professionals, nor did they perform before adoring crowds of spectators. Their activity was pure play and probably more removed from professionalism than that of any of the earlier athletes in history as well.

The Greeks of the Classical Age developed the athletic ideal perhaps more fully than any other culture before or after. In the golden days of Classical Greece, athletes were images of beauty, grace, and perfection. The only political use their great athletic games served related to a general sense of local pride. For the most part, Greek athletes served two basic functions: to perform religious ceremonies to honor the gods, and to portray—in their activities—the ideal citizen.

Most of what we know of the athletes who mirrored these ideals comes from our knowledge of the great festive games that became so popular at this time. First and foremost among these were the *Olympic Games*, which were first held in 776 B.C. and were terminated in 394 A.D. (They were revived in modern and international form in the late 19th century A.D.) The games were held at the foot of Mount Olympus, which (according to Greek myth) was the residence of the greatest of the Greek gods, Zeus.

They were played in homage to Zeus; accordingly, the athletes who participated were obliged to swear allegiance to him and to the rules and honorable conduct codes of the games played in his honor. When an athlete was victorious, it was through the aid of the god he served, and any prizes received came from that same god. Even defeat was a sacred act, symbolizing sacrificial death. In fact, the games were supposedly initiated at the tomb of Pelops, who was believed to have been resurrected from the underworld by the sacrifice of a boy.

Before the advent of the Olympics, other athletic festivals rooted in religious ritual or celebration existed throughout Greece. These were common by at least the ninth century B.C. The Olympic Games themselves were actually an extension of primitive religious festivals that were held at the shrine of Olympia long before. The religious aura remained with the Olympics, as it also did with the Pythian Games held at Delphi in honor of Apollo, the Isthmian Games held at Corinth in honor of Poseidon, and the Nemean Games held in the valley of Nemea in honor of Zeus. These four Panhellenic festivals dominated Greek cultural life in the Classical Age.

But even at the height of the Classical Age, we see the beginnings of great changes in sports and athleticism. Athletes became less and less military figures, and their religious status had become a cliché. The notion of the athlete as the ideal citizen also began to change around this time. Originally, all contestants in the pan-Hellenic festivals were Greek citizens and, as such, they were expected to perform in battle as well as games. The decline of the military character of the games made athletes less likely to be considered ideal warriors. Instead they were idealized for their sheer physical strength, stamina, and grace. Most athletes who participated in the Olympics or other games developed all parts of their body because they participated in most of the events.

In other words, the Classical Greek athlete was not just a runner, or a wrestler, or a pankratiast (a form of combat similar to boxing); he was all of these and more. Being unspecialized, his image had changed from that of a soldier to that of an all-around, well-balanced athlete. He was perfectly conditioned but less and less skilled in combat tactics and weaponry, and more and more skilled in performing in games at the religious festivals.

Fifth-century B.C. Greece had little luxury. As a result, Greek citizen-athletes lived a rugged life in work and in play. Their diet was modest and mostly vegetarian. The common practice of performing nude at athletic events made their skin tough and vibrant. The athlete and the citizen being one and the same, working men and schoolboys alike trained for competition, and all male citizens were expected to participate. From the age of seven and at least until manhood, Greek schoolboys of the Classical era spent many hours daily in physical exercise and training. This they did at the *palaestra* and *gymnasium*, where wrestling and running were the central events. Here, only bathing and dressing were confined by walls; all athletic events were held in the open air.

The ideal athlete of that time has left a lasting impression on later physical trainers, performers, and artists. He reached a level of perfection and beauty virtually unknown before or since. The widespread nature of Classical Greek athleticism was also outstanding. Every male was an athlete for most of his life. Even women, who were barred from attending the contests at Olympia and other places, created their own athletic festival at Heraea. Spartans especially paved the way for women's participation in physical competitions and games. Gymnasiums and palaestrae were among the most common and popular public meeting places of Classical Greece.

The rise of the professional athlete marked the end of the grand amateur tradition. As inducements to enter one festival instead of another, game promoters began to offer attractive prizes. This was contrary to the Olympic tradition of giving nothing but a laurel-wreath crown to its victors.

Meanwhile, the festivals themselves began to entice

commercial interests. Even the Olympics became much more than athletic meetings. *Artists, writers*, and *merchants* were eager to sell their wares at this great assembly of the entire Greek world. Roman writers commonly referred to the Olympic festival as the Olympic "fair," underscoring the trading activity common at the scene. Athletic festivals became so popular because they provided Greek merchants, craftspeople, and the like with a "captive audience" to buy their wares. In this commercial climate, athletes were no longer satisfied with honorary crowns; they began to seek prizes, fame, and glory.

But professionalism was really rooted in the very early stages of the Classical era. Athletes who were victorious at the Panhellenic games had statues erected and hymns of victory recited in their honor. These early contestants were obliged to finance their own victory banquets and had to supply their own entry equipment, such as chariots or armor, in the events themselves. Even so, the victors received a heroes' reception and feast when they returned to their home cities. These honored them and recognized their athletic excellence in the same way that Americans today pay homage to the team that wins the World Series or Super Bowl upon their return to their hometown. The ruler Solon actually offered a reward of 500 drachmae to Athenian victors of Olympic events. Many city-states soon began to grant tax and military exemptions to their local heroes. It has been said that the four great festivals of Greece failed to be religious when the athletes themselves became the objects of worship in place of the gods for whom the games were supposedly held.

The early festival contestants were ideal citizens, who fought for the honor of their home city-states. But this pride also led to division and powerful competition among the cities and the athletes. In the first half century of the Olympic Games, all contestants were Greeks from the western Peloponnesus. Soon afterward the competition had attracted athletes from Sparta, the Isthmus,

Athens, Thebes, and even Greek colonial territories overseas. With the help of mythological genealogies, Macedonians and later Romans were also admitted. Rivalries then became fierce, and in order to win particular events, athletes began to specialize in their training.

But the games were popular. Spectator crowds and stadiums made their first significant historical appearance. Those who now contented themselves with a passive spectator role at the games went to the stadiums, paid admission, and purchased many of the goods offered for sale in and around them. By the early fifth century B.C., "pot hunters"—athletes eager to win trophies—arrived on the scene to exploit the situation. They traveled from city to city, winning prizes while maintaining a rigid, specialized form of training. Their activity further discouraged competition by citizen-athletes, who joined the growing ranks of spectators. The professional athletes were around for a good many years in Classical Greece, but they did not actually dominate the athletic games until the late fifth century B.C. From then on, amateurism survived only in the Olympics.

Greek athletes of the Classical era did not quantify or record their accomplishments in any great detail. But as professionals came to dominate the scene, there was more recording of achievement and comparative statistics. Most of these figures are extremely boastful and hard to believe, however, probably serving as a form of advertisement as much as anything else.

Greek athletes of the Classical Period were probably the first—and, until modern times, the only—to train for athletic events in a scientific and technical manner. They studied the precise techniques and physiological bases of achievement and trained accordingly. The emphasis on training and knowledge led to a kind of class distinction among athletes. Landed peasants obviously could not spend hours at the gymnasium or in physiological studies, which would enable them to play better at the games. The lower classes did become more involved as professionals, however, since they were paid for their efforts and time. In fact, this is the very reason often given by the ancient Greek philosophers for the decline of the art, which they considered athletics to be. Only un-educated and poorly bred people, they said, would accept pay for play—and those who did would certainly know nothing about the science, which athletics was also considered to be. The result, the philosophers charged, was a group of overfed, unevenly developed, proud lugs, who audaciously boasted of their prizes and feats in hope of luring some noblemen into competition.

The new professional athletes developed a new diet. They ate great quantities of everything, especially meat. They overdeveloped the limbs to gain strength for particular events. The ideal athlete of days gone by had had a muscular, developed torso, with supple though strong limbs, which permitted grace and agility. But the professional had notoriously muscle-bound limbs and was clumsy all-around. Corruption accompanied the rise of professionalism. Victories were increasingly bought by politicians or athletes. And some athletes sought financial gain not by winning, but by "taking a fall"—that is, agreeing to lose—in competition.

The reputation of boxers, wrestlers, and pankratiasts indicate another of the effects of professionalism. In the quest to gain attractive prize pots, they became increasingly savage, heavy (there were no weight classifications for any events in ancient Greece), and systematic in their torture of the defeated. At the same time, they abandoned their study of skill, technique, or timing. For example, the wrestlers of the Classical Age—who had performed to music to satisfy their onlookers' (and their own) love of music and harmony—were now replaced by professionals like Sostratus of Sicyon, who defeated his opponents by crushing their fingers rather than through any wrestling skill or technique.

When the Romans began their conquest of Greece in the third century B.C., they found a degenerate society, athletics included. Little was done to repair this situation until the reign of Augustus just before the Christian era. Once Rome had put down the Greeks' final major rebellion in 146 B.C., and Greece became a firm part of the great Roman Empire, Augustus began a massive program of reviving Greek athletics. He recognized the political value of restoring the great games to their original status, the aim being to reduce protest, from the Hellenic city-states of Rome's Eastern Empire. Augustus renewed the games that had fallen by the wayside, restored forgotten events such as Olympic chariot racing, and reestablished the practice of erecting statues to victorious athletes. Festivals once again sprang up throughout the Greek world, probably with more splendor and magnificence than ever before. Rome was prosperous and wealthy, and Augustus invested some of that wealth in cementing relations with the conquered Greeks. He even began a similar festival—the Actian Games—in Rome itself.

For the next two and a half centuries Greek athletes reaped greater rewards for their services than ever before. Even before the golden age of Augustus, Greek athletes had been hired to perform at Roman festivals, celebrations, weddings, and the like. These professionals formed a special class and were endowed with exclusive privileges, which were increased greatly by Augustus. Athletes who were victorious in the Sacred Games were given lifelong pensions as well as complete tax and military exemptions. Specific guidelines for receiving such benefits were written up, and generally these rewards were given only to avowed professionals. Even before Augustus some crude beginnings of unionism existed, developed for the protection of such privileges.

But whatever show of enthusiasm the Romans displayed toward Greek athleticism, it was never much more than that—a show. They were in the midst of building, maintaining, and administering an empire. It was a task that demanded an extraordinary military machine as well as the precision training of practical-minded administrators. There was no taste for the idealism of the Greek philosophers, artists, or athletes.

Most Romans scorned the Greek games, which had lost most of their religious and all of their military character. They ridiculed the strange physiques and poor health of the athletic specialist, and considered competition in the nude to be the foundation of immorality. And who could blame them? The once mighty and powerful Greek Empire had disintegrated and fallen prey to the better-prepared, more efficient, and unified Romans. The Greek athlete-warrior was no match for them.

Roman Athletes

During the days of the mighty Roman Empire, athletes and athleticism took on a very different character, largely influenced by the athletic traditions of Etruria, a key region in central Italy. The Etruscans are frequently thought to have initiated the type of spectacle that was later to become popular in Rome. They were fond of public performances in which large groups of men fought each other, often to the death. This gladiatorial type of contest, dating back to at least the seventh century B.C. in Etruria, was not very well developed, but was popular enough to capture the Romans' interest. The Etruscans were particularly fond of funeral games, since they believed the pleasures derived from them were also shared by the dead. They first introduced chariot racing into Italy, where it was greatly refined and popularized. The most popular activities were combat events, which frequently became rather violent.

By the time Rome finally conquered the Greeks in 146 B.C., it was the greatest power on earth. Soon it had established a society of massive wealth for the upper classes, who had abundant leisure time to spend at the games. As time passed and Rome came to be in firm, stable control of its empire, large numbers of unemployed people began to flock to the capital, where officials became concerned about their numbers and their idleness. To please the wealthy leisure classes and to appease the masses of the unemployed, the Roman elite scrambled to create ample diversion for the hordes of idle thrill-seekers.

Grand festivals were staged, originally of a religious nature, but soon strictly for amusement. They could last for months, anywhere from 60 to 140 days. The Circus Maximus, with crowds of up to 250,000 people, became the scene of the famous chariot and horse races. But "blood" sports were what the crowds really demanded. The Roman Colosseum was the most popular site for these events, which featured gladiatorial combats in which humans and animals alike were slaughtered. One celebration—in honor of Rome's emperor-general Trajan—saw 10,000 gladiators in combat, while 11,000 animals were slain.

The Romans had no taste for Greek athletics. They preferred the blood and combat games (*ludi*) that had military significance. These certainly had little in common with the Greek "contests" (the Greeks never used the term *game*), which featured athletic displays of beauty and grace as well as strength and skill. For the Romans, chariot racing was the most skillful game—but even that was most loved when a lightly constructed chariot traveling at lightning speed suddenly shook loose one of its wooden wheels, and the driver was either smashed into the turf or became tangled in his apparatus and was dragged to his gory death by a team of raging horses. And how much more exciting they considered the teams of gladiators, who killed each other and wild animals in open brawls that featured sword fighting or common bashing with almost any available instrument. Arenas were flooded so that mock naval battles could be staged, and boxing—one of the few true athletic contests enjoyed—was made murderous by the arming of the boxer with a deadly tool, the *caestus*, which had projecting spikes.

The Romans almost totally secularized and greatly bureaucratized the games they inherited from the Greeks and Etruscans. Physical fitness served only as a war exercise, and the Roman games illustrated this. It is difficult to discern any religious motive behind the great battle sponsored by Domitian in 90 A.D., in which groups of dwarves fought against women—but the spectators loved it. These highly popular spectacles required massive organization. When we hear of the central treasury contributing $85 million for such events—and this did not include what must have been considerable supplementary monies from local officials—we can appreciate the necessity of creating a bureaucracy to handle the finances as well as other proceedings associated with them.

Athletes in Roman games performed in a social, political, economic, and cultural environment quite different from that of their Greek and Etruscan predecessors. It was in Rome—with all that money to spend on mass entertainment—that athletes became well paid and provided for. Even before the time of the Roman Empire, some athletes had joined together in organizations, but by the first century A.D. cities throughout the Eastern Roman Empire had full-fledged athletic trade unions called Sacred Synods of the Xystos. By the time of Hadrian in the next century, the most prestigious of the guilds—the Synod of Heracles—was removed to Rome, where it became the central organization of all the synods throughout the empire. The union enjoyed great imperial favor because of its activities, including the organization of traveling games and control over the proceedings of local festivals throughout the Roman colonies. These were important sources of the emperor's political control over the far reaches of his territory as well as over Rome itself.

By the time of the Late Roman Empire, athletes were making unprecedented amounts of money, usually in the form of pensions. Pensions were sometimes awarded as prizes. Athletes won pensions by winning events in the Sacred Games (of which there were a countless number). One athlete is known to have received pensions valued at 2 talents and 3,900 drachmae for two victories over four years. By contrast, skilled laborers at this time received a premium wage of 4 drachmae a day. Successful athletes and their sons also were exempt from public services that even wealthy citizens were obliged to fulfill. They did so well, in fact, that they were frequently the objects of jealousy. Asclepiades of Alexandria, an unbeatable pankratiast and High Priest of the Synod of Heracles, retired at the young age of 25 because he feared personal danger resulting from such jealousy.

Most of the athletes who filled the Colosseum and the Circus Maximus during the gladiatorial festivals were slaves, criminals, or debtors. They were forced to perform in the arenas, where they quickly either lost their lives or gained worthy reputations for themselves. Performers were forced into the arena by whips or hot irons and their fate was often left to the spectators, who made a show of support for either the life or death of the defeated. Nonetheless, some gladiators earned freedom by performing well, and some even returned afterward to gain wealth. Some Roman citizens or warriors, desperate for money or glory, would seek their fortunes through such avenues. Even the half-crazed Emperor Commodus once fought in such a contest, but his victory was certainly contrived.

A closely related occupation was that of *trainer* and *owner* of gladiators. These masters headed schools (*ludi*) of gladiators and hired them out for rather substantial profit during the festivals. While lucrative, their profession was poorly regarded by the rest of the Roman citizenry, and they were seen as sadistic and cruel.

Advertising and record-keeping were important matters for the Roman athlete and performer. The two, of course, were closely related, as was the case with professional Greek athletes beginning in the third century B.C. Games and festivals were widely advertised, with the corresponding records of contestants used to arouse the excitement of would-be spectators. Prominently displayed on the advertising pamphlets for gladiatorial shows was the name of the official who was kind enough to "give" the games. Spectators received free admission because of his generosity. The giver was usually present at the games he sponsored, and he was often turned to as the ultimate judge in matters of dispute on the field.

Professional Roman athletes, as highly paid and organized as they were, were rarely Romans themselves. In marked contrast to the original Greek ideal of the athleticism of the amateur-citizen, Roman athletes began receiving such great amounts of money for performing that the average citizen could not compete, being unable to devote enough time and training to the craft. Even the Olympics—which always remained amateur in ideal but allowed professional entries by the Late Roman Empire—came to offer a solid gold, rather than laurel-wreath, crown. Greek citizens thought it foolish for merchants or artisans to work so hard at their businesses that they had no time for the gymnasium. But Roman citizens thought it foolish to train so hard in athletics

The close connection between military battle and sports is clearly seen in the gladiatorial combat of the Romans. (From Men: A Pictorial Archive From Nineteenth-Century Sources, *by Jim Harter, Dover, 1980)*

when there were fields to plow and wars to win. As a result, athletes in Rome became two things: entertainers and symbols of militarism. The idea was that industrious (and even idle) Roman citizens ought to be treated to watching the "barbarians" kill and compete with each other. Athletics, while often lucrative, was considered below the dignity of Roman citizens. Their only avowed interest in the spectacle was to observe the mock military strategies, maneuvers, and tactics employed in the gladiatorial and athletic games.

Athletes, to please their audiences, were at once heroes and second-class citizens. The greatest of the performers probably received genuine and widespread acclaim and honor, but the rest were despised for their failure or mediocrity. Athletes were well compensated for their displays, but their training was long and bitter. They were forced to overdevelop parts of the body—especially the limbs—to an unsightly and unhealthy degree. Their diets were grossly unbalanced, and with all their overexercising and overeating, they seldom lived past what was considered middle age at that time. Those who did were beset with poor health, crippled with wounds, prone to disease, and sometimes had bodies too muscle-bound to perform daily activities. Specialization had reached its height, as Roman citizens, watching others fight for prizes, stood aloof from the fray themselves. Athleticism had changed dramatically. From the earliest days of Mesopotamian, Egyptian, and Greek games, athletes had performed primarily for themselves. By the last days of the Roman Empire, the highly polished professional athletes no longer performed for themselves, but for the spectators. They were no longer athletes in sacred festivals, but *performers* in secular circuses.

Medieval Athletes

Medieval Europe was marked by a decline of central political authority. The Western world was carved up by petty lords, who created small kingdoms for themselves out of their huge land holdings and controlled the lives of peasants and nobles alike. This feudal life was local and provincial. Most people were born and died in one manor and never ventured further. The one authority that loomed greater than the local lord was the Catholic Church. The medieval church offered the greatest hope for average people—the promise of freedom from toil and bondage in the afterlife, as well as spiritual stimulation and even a sort of education in their earthly lives.

The history of professional sport and games during this period has gone practically unwritten—and for good reason. As the Christian era replaced the Roman, athletes lost most of their respectability. As a result of pressure from the church, gladiatorial games were abolished in Rome by the Emperor Constantine I in 325 A.D. The matter was not so easily settled, though, since they again had to be stopped during the reign of Honorious, from 393 to 423 A.D.

The role of athletes was considered an extension of the old pagan rites so abhorred by the Roman Catholic Church. Also, they were seen primarily as *players*. Since play was viewed as worthless frivolity, the athletic role was regarded as not useful, and even anti-Christian, in the sense that it diverted Christian athletes from their more serious concerns in life. The Roman Catholic Church often pronounced that God had more profound business in mind for His subjects in this world than idle hours in play. By the Late Middle Ages—roughly the 14th to 16th centuries—play or sport could hardly be detected, except within a military training framework. Only with the advent of the Reformation in the 16th and 17th centuries, were religious restrictions on play and sport somewhat relaxed in Europe. (But in Puritan America, play was suppressed as never before.)

Games, contests, and athletics continued to exist into the Middle Ages, as they had in nearly every known culture from the earliest of times. But after gladiatorial contests were banned, there is virtually no trace of organized sports for centuries. There is hardly any mention of sport or games from the fall of Rome until about the middle of the 11th century, when the Age of Chivalry revived an interest in physical activity, which had been long suppressed. Then there was a renewal of physical training and contests of display. The *tournament*, with its military games such as jousting, archery, and wrestling, came to the forefront of what may be considered a mild athletic revival.

The contests of this time were restricted almost totally to militaristic ones. The principal reason for this—and for the "athletic" revival itself—was that the feudal society of the period led to almost constant local warfare. The soldiers, or *knights* as they were called, were drawn from the upper classes, if only because the peasants were so grossly unhealthy from their long, inhumanely arduous toil in the fields. But even the nobles were found to be

Medieval jousting tournaments once again combined athletics with military prowess. (By Albrecht Dürer, early 16th century)

generally unfit for the demanding task of steady warfare. New programs of physical fitness, then, were initiated for the sole purpose of developing a stronger race of knights. Out of this military zeal was born the tournament.

The physical training of knights did not compare with that of the Greeks or even the Romans. They did not train their bodies with intelligent programs of exercise or diet. They emphasized almost exclusively the art of warfare and the manipulation of weapons, such as lances, bows and arrows, and swords. Participants in tournaments were carefully screened regarding such qualifications as social status and skill. Once admitted they participated in one-on-one competitions early in the tournament, and in massive mock wars toward the end. They often lost their lives or were seriously maimed during these games. Not infrequently more knights were killed as "players" or "athletes" in tournaments and jousts, than as warriors in real combat. Measures were taken to reduce the violence and to bring more order to the proceedings, but the tournament remained basically intact until the 16th century.

Like warrior-athletes of earlier times, knights were professional soldiers rather than professional athletes. Prizes were given, however, to those who excelled in the military games, and honors were bestowed on all participants. Before the activities began, the combatants were announced to the ladies and nobles of the audience by heralds and elaborate fanfare, as the magnificently armored knights made their gala entrance onto the field atop grandly dressed horses.

The knights who competed in such "sport" were highly revered. They competed in partial fulfillment of the duties of their high social standing and to affirm the ideals of chivalry. Though at times reminiscent of the Greeks' ideal athlete-citizen, they were really quite different. They were symbols of law, order, and decency in a world that for centuries had been ruled and ransacked by various tribes of barbarians who cared little for any of those things. The knights' role cannot be identified with the democratic notion of "citizenship"; rather they were patronizing figures who protected the public and executed the will of the feudal lord, much as *police officers* now enforce the laws of their respective societies.

Knights were on display when engaged in tournament games. They especially took pride in close one-on-one combat in which they showed off their military skills and physical prowess. They had become heroes in a society desperately seeking symbols of law and order, and high standards of conduct. In ancient Greece, hero worship had led to athletic professionalism, but this was not to be in the Early Middle Ages.

By the end of the Early Middle Ages, feudal society was beginning to break down as towns and cities developed, and a new sort of middle class of burghers (prosperous town-dwellers), merchants, and artisans arose. The new class had few ties to the feudal lordship or the toil of the land. Oriented as it was toward profit and business, it was more secular in its outlook. These middle classes were involved in playing games that more closely resembled modern sports, although these games were simple pastimes and purely recreational.

The church attempted to sanctify the games by providing religious significance for them, but this was not to be. In truth, they were so disorganized that they are more properly referred to as folk games. The most popular of these was *la soule*, a primitive form of soccer and football, among other things. Entire villages would engage in the game, and there was little differentiation between participant and spectator. The object, apparently, was for one village to kick a round ball into the opposing village, whose players were, of course, trying to kick the same ball in the opposite direction. The game may have originally been started by the clergy as part of a religious ceremony, but it was quickly secularized to the fullest degree.

Records show that monarchs opposed the folk game (which came to be called *football*) because it was—as

England's King Edward complained on April 13, 1314, in his formal ban of the game—an activity "from which many evils might arise which God forbid." It was a crude game, which was terribly brutal, causing countless injuries. The game was often used as a license for violence, as people settled old disputes under the guise of sport. Nonparticipants were terrified and often stampeded, as shops closed and the fearful and weak took to hiding. In the 12th century King Henry II had banned *futballe* because he had feared that his subjects were becoming obsessed with the frivolous sport, which detracted from their compulsory archery practice. Players were threatened with prison terms, as were owners of land that was used to accommodate the games. Obviously, the Early Middle Ages offered little climate for the development of sport even as an amateur undertaking, much less as a profession.

Renaissance and Reformation Athletes

The 14th, 15th, and early 16th centuries are well known as the European Renaissance. This was a period of a "rebirth" of interest in the Classical Age of Greece and Rome. There was new interest in education and Greek and Roman art, literature, philosophy, and athletics. Teachers began to stress—as had the Greeks—the importance of the total development of the person, which included physical as well as intellectual, spiritual, and artistic development.

Renaissance Europeans revived games to a great extent. A new intellectual and educational movement called *humanism* stressed making the most of human capabilities and revived interest in classical learning. This spurred interest in sport and play as a matter of good health as well as a recreational diversion from strict intellectual and religious training. Vittorino da Feltre, who died in 1446, became one of the first modern *educators* to call for physical training and exercise as an integral part of any "total" educational curriculum. He is considered one of the most important figures in the history of *physical education.*

The period from the 14th through 17th centuries, then, was conspicuous for the development of games and sport. Even the clergy were involved in the revival of games. They welcomed the opportunity to offer more civilized alternatives to spectacles such as *la soule* (football). They led the way to the creation of a new ball game, *jeu di paume* (game of the hand). It was similar to modern *handball,* but then developed into *paddle-ball* and finally court *tennis. Ice skating* came to be widely practiced in northern countries, such as Scandinavia, England, and Holland, and by 1642 the Scots had organized the (presumably amateur) Skating Club of Edinburgh. James II of England banned the playing of *golfe* in 1457, because it distracted his subjects from what he regarded as more worthwhile projects, such as training in archery.

While most of these sports were played only by aristocrats, the lower-class people continued to play *football, soccer,* and other rough-and-tumble field sports that did not require special equipment or a particular setting, such as a palace court or churchyard. Large numbers of people could play these games, which generally had no limits on the number of participants. The aristocrats, of course, thought the sports of the lower classes were crude and barbaric, and preferred their

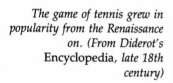

The game of tennis grew in popularity from the Renaissance on. (From Diderot's Encyclopedia, *late 18th century)*

finer games. Monarchs often tried to prevent the playing of the lower-class sports, but by and large they continued to develop.

Games of chance became particularly popular as people tried their hand at betting on *horse racing, dog racing*, and *lawn bowls*. As early as 1299, a group of bowlers formed the Southampton Town Bowling Club in England. King Henry VIII outlawed "the game of bowles" in 1511, declaring it to be "an evil because the alleys are operated in conjunction with saloons, or dissolute places, and because bowling has ceased to be a sport, and rather a form of vicious gambling." Similar laws were from time to time passed against dog and horse racing, although dog racing in England was commonly called "the Sport of Queens," indicating its royal favor. Horse racing was also enjoyed by British royalty, who themselves were the exclusive breeders of Arabian and Moroccan purebreds (known as the "Royal Horses") for centuries, dating back to the early 12th-century reign of Henry I.

The most popular and intriguing sports of the Renaissance, though, were those that had developed from military functions. *Fencing* was foremost, having originally been developed as a way for gentlemen to settle disputes in duels to the death. If a gentleman were challenged to such a duel, he was obliged to accept or lose his honor and dignity. Training in this sport, obviously, became regular and virtually universal among the upper classes in Western Europe.

Boxing and *wrestling* became extremely popular, too. The clergy developed boxing, in its modern form, as a less drastic alternative to fencing duels. Wrestling was a major event at tournaments, and international contests drew intense interest from rival monarchs. In the 16th century, King Francis I, upset by the way his French wrestlers were being beaten by the English at one such match, impetuously grabbed Henry VIII—his royal opponent—and began a royal wrestling match in public.

With the Protestant Reformation of the 16th and 17th

centuries came a new feeling of people's power to direct and control their destinies to some degree. By the 17th century John Locke was even challenging both the divine right of kings to legislate for their subjects and the long-accepted notion that governments were designed by God and not humans.

These were revolutionary ideas in revolutionary times. Religious wars were being fought everywhere, while burghers began the "good works" of making money and improving their social, financial, and political standing in the secular world. An important part of the Protestant work ethic was this—that God's grace, His predetermined election of those chosen people who would be granted salvation, was evident by their good works and worldly success. Eventually capitalism was born of the new work ethic, and subsequently the Industrial Revolution.

During the exhilarating times of the Reformation, sport continued to grow. Most athletes were aristocrats who followed rigorous training schedules and often won prizes for successful competitions. Schools of fencing were established throughout Europe. *Masters* earned a living by teaching their craft to others, and some of the best fencers themselves earned prize money in competitions at touring carnivals. Toward the middle of the 17th century, *prizefighting* with bare fists became well known in England; contestants were usually of the lower classes. As early as 1400 a professional guild of *tennis masters* or *coaches* was formed in France. While there are few records of *lawn bowlers* earning money, they almost certainly did, owing to large amounts of money involved in related side bets. The training of both dogs and horses may have involved some professionalism, as well, with most of it carried on within royal confines. Prizes were awarded for horse racing as early as the 16th century.

In general, these athletes were nonprofessionals, however, and were regarded very highly only if their skill was particularly functional, as with combative events. Clergy and monarchy alike complained about the idleness and evil of sport and game, yet most athletes in this period were aristocrats engaged in the "finer" sports. Tennis and fencing were "court games" played at the palace or church courtyard. They were generally performed for the enjoyment, exercise, and training of the participants. Spectators, even in the games that were played by commoners, were not usually an important element of the sporting event. The tournament and racing spectacles were notable exceptions in this respect.

As the 18th century approached, athletes as a class did not exist as they had in Classical times. Sport itself was far from the athletic precision and beauty of the glorious days of ancient Greece. Yet a fairly new phenomenon was beginning to evolve, as games and athletics were combined into more organized forms of what we now call *sports*. Scarcely any records were kept of athletes themselves or their accomplishments, however, since it was the event and not the individual participants that gave rise to the popularity of the wide variety of sports that cropped up at this time. Athletes, by now, had completely lost all vestige of religious importance. They were either gentry receiving a "full" education, warriors training to improve combat skills, or commoners seeking relief from the toil of the fields, much to the disgust of the aristocracy.

Athletes of this period were not specialized, and the thought of a class of athletes who actually "played" as a profession ran counter to the new industrious climate sparked largely by the Protestant work ethic. Spectatorship itself was little developed, since it, too, was seen as an evil form of vagrancy. Athletes, then, were essentially employed as a means to other ends, either religious, commercial, or political. There were few professionals, and even fewer professional guilds to protect this class. There was also strict segregation along class lines; common athletes did not compete with nobles except in the most extreme cases.

The rising business class, which had hardly existed before the Renaissance, was interested in trying its luck at the races and in sponsoring fairs that were generally commercial, but featured athletic events. Athletes were relatively insignificant performers in a larger arena that might include a clothiers' fair in Brussels, or one of the Queen's horse races in England. Most who earned a living through their skill did so as *masters* or *coaches* of young, aristocratic amateurs, who wished to excel in the more popular court games, such as billiards, lawn bowls, tennis, and fencing. Such coaches taught either in schools or by private assignment, much as a tutor would teach academic skills.

Athletes Outside Europe

In Eastern cultures, sport seems to have been almost totally of a military nature. The Samurai warriors of Japan were famous for their expertise in the martial arts. Although they undoubtedly engaged in sporting contests, it seems doubtful that prizes were sought. Under the Tokugawa shogunate (1603-1867), the Samurai did begin to receive government pensions for their service, but even this payment was in return for military rather than athletic performance. Perhaps the only real professionalism here can be found with the class of *Sumo wrestlers*, who commonly performed for the emperor and at public events. These wrestlers were perhaps spectacles more than athletes, averaging somewhere between 300 and 400 pounds in weight.

In the Near East, military concerns related to the forceful spreading of Islam also dictated whatever sport may be said to have existed. Early in the seventh century, the revered prophet Mohammed greatly popularized *horseback riding* in his fervent desire to create the world's greatest armed force. Indeed, the Arabs became some of the most skilled riders ever known. Again, contests certainly developed out of the stringent forms of military horse-riding training that warriors received, but no professional *riders* appear to have come to the fore.

Meanwhile, in India, the game of *polo*, thought to have been invented by other great equestrians—the ancient Persians—was greatly developed. Again, though, no professional activity seems to have issued from this interest.

Many Native Americans engaged in sporting activity for centuries before Columbus's discovery of the New World. These sports almost always had purely religious and cultic formats. The Apaches of North America's Southwest played ball games that were related to solar and lunar worship in conjunction with elaborate fertility rites. The Native Americans of the northern Plains had an elaborate system of strictly ritualistic and ceremonial games and events that were used to entreat the gods for everything from curing sickness and prolonging life to demon exorcism. Wrestling and hunting "exercises" seem to have been almost universal among the peoples of both American continents. The best-documented case of sport as ritual is the Mayan-Aztec ball-court game that many authorities believe to have been the predecessor of *jai-alai*, which was developed later by the Spaniards. An elaborate solar-lunar mythology was ceremoniously mimicked as part of the game. The ball courts were located within the temple complex, as was the beautifully preserved one at Chichén Itzá in Yucatán, Mexico. The contest actually involved human sacrifice to the gods, as the losers were doomed for their failure in the "game." After Hernando Cortés and his Spanish Conquistadors invaded Aztec lands in 1519, the game was banned as a heathen display.

Games in these societies were not organized into sports, nor were they played by a special class of athletes. They involved total community participation and were serious business. In North America, for example, *lacrosse* was developed as a war-training exercise. But with the arrival of Europeans, particularly the English and Dutch in northeastern North America, both organized and professional sports flooded the old Native American homelands, beginning as early as the mid-19th century.

Changing Times

But it was in Western Europe that sport was given its impetus for development. It was here that the Renaissance and Reformation had introduced new humanistic and scientific ideals that would soon lead to a new industrial world and the golden age of professional sports. The ideas of enlightenment, invention, and finally industrialization dominated the 18th century. As people began to claim their "natural" human rights, a wave of revolutions changed the political, economic, and social face of the West.

The vast changes that gripped the world also brought sport to greater public attention than it had known since the days of the early Greeks and Romans. Along with the industrialization and democratization of the West came a new powerful middle class of laborers and businesspeople. This class was not spread out in rural villages, as the commoners and peasants of earlier times had been; its members were congregated in large numbers in central urban areas. They did not toil in the fields from sunup to sundown, but gradually gained more leisure time in the form of shorter work days, shorter work weeks, and paid vacations and holidays. Adults and children, as well, still worked long, grueling hours for little pay, by today's standards. Still, with increasing leisure and income, people spent more time participating in—and later watching—sports.

An outgrowth of the new structure of society was the universal education movement. As increasing numbers of young boys and girls began to attend school, organized recreation in the form of games and sports became common. By the early 1800's some Western governments were making "physical education" a compulsory feature of the public school curriculum. Originally this was to fulfill national requirements for citizens physically prepared for "labor and defense." But it was not long before physical education strayed from so sober a course.

The British Empire is generally considered to have set the foundations for the great age of professional sport, which was to begin toward the end of the 19th century. This sprang in part from a revival of interest in the Greek athletic idealism, especially in the British public schools—which in America would be called *private* schools. By the 19th century, these were churning out an elite group of young men with a love of sport. As they spread throughout the British Empire, they brought with them their enthusiasm for sport. These were Christian schools, and "muscular Christianity" was the name commonly given to the export of British sports such as *cricket* and *soccer*. British athletes saw themselves as bearers of a better way of life to the "heathen" of India, Africa, and the West Indies. With their "muscular Christianity," they were establishing themselves as model patriots, soldiers, and citizens. In fact, throughout the 19th-century world, Western athletes represented a patriotic idealism in a world of growing nationalism and pride in worldly achievement. So the new sports movement in the British schools influenced the history of sport throughout the world.

A passion for sport also grew in the new industrialized urban societies. As people moved from the fields to factory labor, they became separated from their rural traditions as well as from healthful physical exercise and fresh air. Sports filled this void. Some played as active amateurs. But gradually, as athletes became more professional and specialized, more and more people became simply spectators. The working classes were eager to be entertained after long hours in the factory. The urban areas provided a large, concentrated potential audience upon which organized, professional sports would soon come to depend.

In England's New World colonies, the Puritans had kept alive the ascetic ideals of work and self-denial until the 18th century. In early New England only strictly utilitarian sports such as hunting were encouraged. However, games and pleasurable sport were played at taverns, which evolved as centers for such "trespass sports." In the Mid-Atlantic and Southern colonies sport was—as in England and the rest of Europe—the pastime of the leisure aristocracy. In the frontier regions, the force of organized churches was not as great as in the Eastern colonies. There taverns and gambling were tremendously popular.

The Rise of Professionals

To a considerable extent, it was America's great push westward in the mid-19th century that developed the sporting spirit—and gave birth to the unbridled professionalization of athletics. The combination of rapid urbanization and massive industrialization led to large numbers of people who wanted to escape the textile mills and other monotonous, unhealthy, and confined occupations. These frustrated city-dwellers often traveled westward, where they celebrated their freedom by reveling in sports and games. By the early 19th century, American athletes were seen as upholding the pride of the new nation that had recently overthrown the most powerful empire in the world—Britain. They were brash and determined to win.

Even so, athletes were not considered a bona fide professional group until at least the middle of the 19th century. It was at this time, with the United States in the lead, that expert *players* began to gain recognition as *workers* entitled to payment and pensions, not just occasional prizes. The emerging professional became a specialist, as sport itself became organized into a coherent display. After the American Civil War, sports became commercialized as a form of entertainment for the growing numbers of leisure-time spectators. They became specialized, mass-produced, and nationally marketed. Professional athletes were part of the package—they were what this new flock of consumers was paying to see.

The shift took place gradually, and at different times

for different sports. Baseball provides a classic example. Early baseball clubs were strictly amateur and local. But as teams began to travel and earn prizes, profit motivation became more prevalent. In 1867 the National Association of Base Ball Players (founded in 1865) had a membership of 237 amateur clubs. And already, gate receipts had become so attractive that clubs were seeking members from outside the community, which went against their local and "player" constitution.

In 1867 the most successful amateur club—the National Base Ball Club of Washington—toured the nation, paying its own expenses along the way. But in the same year the Excelsiors of Chicago existed as a semiprofessional "club." By 1869 the Cincinnati Red Stockings were openly professional. Team members pursued baseball as a total vocation, being paid for their time, travel, and talent. Although the Red Stockings were called a club, they had no strictly local membership

Baseball was one of the first team sports to be played by professionals, paid for their efforts. (By W.P. Snyder, from Harper's Weekly, May 8, 1886)

and were cemented by a group of participants who sought not conventional recreation, or time out from work, but full-time payment for services rendered, thereby making work out of play and vocation out of avocation. *Baseball players* received increasing pay and publicity after the National Association of Base Ball Players was organized in 1871.

In the 20th century, developments in transportation and communication brought sports throughout the Western world. Football, basketball, golf, wrestling, automobile racing, horse racing, tennis, ice hockey, and many others joined the ranks of successful professional sports. The profit motives of entrepreneurs—independent owners—combined with the frustration of modern spectators in their attempts to cope with a world of ever-increasing automation and anonymity. The result was an enthusiasm for professional, organized sports that was unprecedented in the history of athletics.

Modern athletes became professionals paid because they delivered entertainment as well as displaying skill. Since their success is based solely on individual talent, old established class lines have eroded in sports. The gentleman-athlete of the 19th century has given way to a new hero—the ghetto kid who fights his way into the limelight of the sporting world. Contemporary athletes have been recognized for their capabilities rather than their social status. This has tended to diminish earlier sharp class, racial, and sexual distinctions in sports, although problems still remain.

In recent times, Blacks have begun to participate in the rewards of the athletic profession. Early baseball clubs had restricted class as well as racial enrollments, and Blacks were forced to form their own leagues. Then, in 1947, Jackie Robinson became the first Black professional major league baseball player in the United States by joining the Brooklyn Dodgers. Today, there are countless Blacks in all major league sports. Nonetheless, there are still complaints that Blacks are restricted to stereotyped positions within their respective sports. It is often mentioned that most Black football players are linemen and running backs, but rarely quarterbacks, and that Black baseball players are usually outfielders, but rarely pitchers. And very few Blacks are given management opportunities in professional sports. Women athletes have fared worse than Blacks and are still excluded from most of the professional arenas. Nonetheless, their amateur standing has been improving steadily, especially in the socialist countries. With continual court battles and suits, women have succeeded in opening doors traditionally closed tight in their faces. In 1978, for example, Cathy "Cat" Davis of Texas won a string of court battles enabling her to become the first professional female boxer.

As sports have become increasingly profitable and organized, so have athletic guilds. There are an endless array of contemporary professional athletic unions that serve to protect the enormous salaries and rights of its members. As athletes become better paid, however, they also seem to be more disenchanted with their professions. Many complain that they are forced to portray stereotypical images both on the field and off, and are deprived of their right to be individualistic and distinctive. More seriously, professional athletes have very short careers, and often are left with painful and debilitating injuries for the rest of their lives. Although such complaints are not new, they have increasingly been forced upon the attention of management and spectators. The 1981 American professional baseball players' strike, for example, lasted half of the season and caused team owners to lose millions of dollars in gate receipts. As fans and players offered opposing views on the merits of the strike, the oldest paradox in sports emerged as the central issue: how can people "play" as a profession? And if they do, how can they expect sympathy for their labor troubles from people who "really work"—that is, the typical fan?

Another modern feature of the occupation is the enthusiastic and precise quantification of athletes' accomplishments. In the sacred atmosphere within which sports were played in ancient times, records were considered of little value, since only the event itself—a gift to the gods—was ultimately significant. But today an athlete's exploits seem to have value only if they (and in some spectacular cases, the athlete himself) are "immortalized" through the eternal comparison of statistics.

The importance of records and statistics has had a sharp impact on modern athletes. Their salaries are determined largely on end-of-the-year statistical analyses of their performance. As statistics become increasingly refined, their interpretation becomes less objective, and more contract disputes are rooted in just this variance of interpreting the "stats." It was rather revolutionary to learn that a baseball player was hitting .333—that is, that for every 1,000 times at bat, he had 333 hits. But beyond that rather straightforward statistic, many a .333 hitter must now explain at contract time why he only hit .212 with runners in scoring position, thereby altering the ultimate value of his overall .333 average. He may retort that in games in which his team was behind at the time, and with runners in scoring position, his average was .368; or that in the last three innings (which many people in sports think are more important than the first six) his comparative average was .372. And this is only the beginning of the confusion in attempting to definitively "score" a player by his performance. Yet in today's world of athletics, numbers are considered almost sacred in determining an athlete's exact, precise worth.

The comparative merits of various athletic training systems have become points of sharp controversy in our times. Most professional athletes have willingly chosen to become athletes at a young age, and so have trained since high-school age or earlier toward this end. Unlike the ancient Greeks, a minor (though varying) portion of society undertakes rigorous physical development and only a small number become professional athletes. And unlike the "amateur" athletes in modern socialist countries, the professionals in the West are not usually trained according to specifically regulated programs until they are well into their careers. Some socialist governments have underwritten pioneer research projects in physiology, and their athletes have benefitted from these.

Although physical training in the West is not the science it is in some socialist countries, the quality of performance does not seem to vary considerably at the professional level. Western athletes are generally as big and strong and healthy as in any in the world. Ancient athletes used to advertise in order to obtain qualified competition and to excite spectators enough to come out and see them. Today's athletes not only promote their own talents, but also use their fame to sell products for others through the mass medium of advertising.

Another subtler form of advertising—personal publicity—is also used by athletes for a variety of reasons. Mohammed Ali used it successfully in professional boxing in the 1960's and 1970's to stimulate a new enthusiasm in a sport that had been somewhat forgotten by the public and press alike. Some managers and players try to make themselves "attractions," not so much for their skill (though they may have that, too) but for their antics or personalities.

Images of the Athlete

Hero worship and personal identification have given a special image to modern-day professional athletes. They are sometimes seen as simple, rugged men who exist with nature and, just as they control the physical movements of their own bodies within space and time, they are imagined to control their entire destiny for the moment and forever. Sometimes "toughness" is part of that image. Babe Ruth may have died, but his 60 home runs in 1927 live on in the record books and in his legend, which has been reverently passed on to succeeding generations through a lineage of his disciples and worshippers. No one tells "Mean" Joe Greene—long a mammoth lineman of the Pittsburgh Steelers—what to do, the hero worshipers fantasize. No one tells him to punch a time card at 8 A.M., or to pick up the groceries on the way home. In acting out this role and playing up to this image, the modern athlete achieves a kind of immortality in a secular world.

Rather than being simply a tool of corruptors and exploiters, then, modern athletes also reflect a new idealism that is found in both Marxist and capitalist nations. This may be summarized by the term *competitive*. Athletes are most attractive to modern spectators when they are fulfilling their role as supreme competitors. This may help explain why the business elite are such ardent fans, and why athletes themselves are often politically active, rather than passive. Modern athletes are the model of competition in our era. They are out to win at any cost. They may appear to be courteous, but they are often ruthless and determined to attain their goal. In many countries, athletes are considered to be symbolic of national pride, unity, strength, and supremacy. The result is some widely divergent perceptions of what an athlete is.

Athletes can also be seen as representing a romantic rejection of modern society. They provide psychological and emotional pastoral relief from modern urban life. The athletes work in a profession which allows them a romantic freedom unfamiliar to most modern workers. They deal in a service and a product, as commercial sport certainly is. Yet as producers, they do not deliver a factory product which is mass produced. Instead they deal, like a craftsperson, in personally produced goods which are probably more truly *their own* than most other products which issue from the modern economy.

Modern athletes are also performers and, like performing artists, have the opportunity to "present themselves" to others, avoiding the anonymity that other workers suffer. Athletes themselves speak of their work in terms such as "liberating," "unity of movement and aim," and "discovering oneself." The fan who sees the athlete as a symbol of freedom and individualism is probably observing more than a mere public image. Most professional athletes are proud of and happy with their occupations, and go to great extremes of personal and financial sacrifice to enter and stay in them.

Most of the contemporary professional development of sports and athletes has occurred in the West, particularly in the United States, but professionalism also exists elsewhere, increasingly influenced by the Western model. In most parts of the world *soccer* is the most popular sport, with professionals as well as amateurs playing around the world. *Track and field* (frequently called *athletics*) is globally the second most popular type of sport. Neither is as important in the United States, and track and field events throughout the world are primarily the concern of amateur athletes. There are relatively few professional non-Western athletes. Those of the great socialist countries are technically considered to be amateurs.

The two classes of athletes—the amateur and the professional—are sometimes hard to distinguish. Technically the amateur athlete pursues sport as an avocation (as play) and the professional athlete pursues it as a vocation (as work). But the line between the two is decidedly blurry. Various cultural perceptions of athletes and their role in the social order have added to the confusion. This is probably nowhere more evident than in the entry qualifications of the modern Olympic Games, revived in 1896.

Essentially classical in their approach, modern Olympic officials have barred from competition any athlete who has ever earned money in sports competition. American athlete Jim Thorpe was even stripped of his two Olympic gold medals, won at Stockholm in 1912, because he had inadvertently accepted pay from a professional baseball team in an isolated incident. Yet American collegiate athletes, who earn scholarships (including tuition, room, and board) and—to the dismay of various college sports associations—many other "gifts" and benefits in return for their performances, are readily admitted to Olympic contests. The same is true of athletes from many socialist countries, where specialized training is made available at an early age to those who display physical prowess. Athletes in such countries are often trained at government expense. Soviet families even receive monetary compensation while their child is enrolled at a "sports school." They also receive special status with respect to citizenship and military enrollment. But they, too, are common figures at the Olympics.

The confusion between amateur and professional is not a new one. Its roots can be traced back at least to the glorious days of Greek athletics. It is no easy matter to discern through the sports history literature which athletes were amateurs and which were professional. But, in today's sports the distinction has been rigorously legislated by groups like the International Amateur Athletic Federation, the United States Amateur Athletic Union (AAU), the U.S. National Association of Intercollegiate Athletics (NAIA), the Amateur Athletic Association of England, and the International Olympic Committee. Still, the distinction between professional and amateur poses more of a problem today than ever before, perhaps because of attempts to define it so strictly.

Professional athletes today take on an extremely complicated task. They must appear to be sportspeople in the tradition of the gallant amateur, but must equally be showpeople in order to entertain the public spectators, who seek thrills and excitement beyond proper execution of technique. Professional athletes must also conform to the ideals of the society in which they perform. If they fail to do that, at least in some measure, they risk being charged with presenting an unbecoming image for those who idealize sport heroes. Amateur athletes do not need a group of spectators to witness, remember, record, and allegorize the sporting event. Professional athletes not only need such spectators, but need to communicate with and entertain them.

Athletes may find professional work either as members of sports teams or as individuals who perform without the assistance of fellow players. *Bowlers, weight lifters*, and *skiers* are examples of individual athletes who compete against each other in one-on-one competitions. Probably the most popular athletes within this classification are *boxers* and *tennis players*, while *bullfighters* in Mexico and Spain are among the highest-paid individual athletes in the world. Sometimes individual athletes join within others to play *teams* or *doubles* in particular sports. Bowlers and *swimmers* frequently perform in teams, while tennis players sometimes engage in doubles competitions. But this class of athletes usually competes as individuals.

Some individual athletes are closer to being pure entertainers rather than athletes. *Wrestlers* provide a classic example of this, feigning holds, takedowns, and incredible acts of sadism and torture against their rivals. While failing to provide authentic shows of athleticism, they do provide their viewers with ample entertainment in acting out stereotypical and identifiable roles, among which good and evil are the most common.

Professional golfers rely on their individual skill, expertise, and a bit of luck. (From Men: A Pictorial Archive From Nineteenth-Century Sources, *by Jim Harter, Dover 1980)*

Bullfighters or *matadors* are also frequently identified with similarly dramatic roles, and the ritual and ceremony involved are often broken down into three stages, which are likened to the three acts of a play. As with ancient and primitive ritualistic sport, though, the action itself is for real and the results are for keeps. Matadors and their attendant *toreros* (assistants on horseback) bear the closest similarity to the ancient Roman gladiators in terms of role expectations and performance. Unlike the gladiator, though, bullfighters are practically deified by the adoring throng, which pays to see them do their job or perform their ritual. Successful matadors often live like princes following their retirement. Bullfighting is extremely popular in Mexico and much of Latin America, and it is the national sport of Spain. Although bullfighters date back to at least 12th-century Arabia, the first matadors to fight on foot rather than on horseback lived in the 18th century.

Professional *ice skaters*, too, are usually employed to perform rather than actually compete with other skaters. *Skiers, fencers, weight lifters*, and *swimmers* also perform sheerly for entertainment at times, but they also engage in competitions for prizes. Even professional boxers often go on exhibition tours, where the competition is secondary to the entertainment value of their show. Muhammad Ali made showmanship antics a cliché in modern boxing, even during serious prize competition. The *martial arts* are professionally practiced by exhibitionists and contestants in Asia, and many masters of the martial arts are employed throughout the world in teaching their craft to others.

The history of individual sports is much longer and richer than that of team sports. Today, the individual athlete represents clear class distinctions. *Tennis players* present the most stereotypical image of playing an aristocratic game; their heritage is derived from the great palace version of *court tennis*, which dates back many centuries. The fact that professional tennis remains dominated by upperclass Whites is often attributed to the long, individual, and expensive enterprise of training young tennis players. On the other side of the street stands the *boxer*, the model of the poor, street-wise kid who pulls himself out of the ghetto by learning to fight. Although boxers and tennis players often come from opposite ends of the social spectrum, they are both among the most popular and highly paid professionals in sport today. They both seem to attract an increasingly diverse audience, representing a considerable ethnic, social, sexual, and economic crossover.

Team sports have been a relatively new phenomenon in the history of professional sport. Baseball, basketball, and football are the most popular American team sports, while cricket, rugby, and soccer are extremely popular in most other areas of the world, including Africa, Latin America, and Asia. Ice hockey is particularly popular in Canada, as is jai-alai in Mexico and Latin America. Baseball is the major team sport in Japan.

Team players were almost nonexistent before the early 19th-century professionalization of cricket in England and before U.S. baseball became professionalized by the Cincinnati Red Stockings in 1869. After that, others followed suit rapidly. Team sports opened many more professional slots for athletes to fill, as teams joined to form leagues and leagues expanded in size and popularity. The arrival of television in the mid-20th century gave team sports fantastic visibility as spectatorship reached unprecedented levels.

Team play is often thought to have evolved from the American frontier experience, in which cooperation was necessary to survive the wilds. It directly contrasts with the European tradition of the individual, aristocratic player. Certainly the team phenomenon has had its greatest impact in the United States. The "team player" is often thought of as a symbol of socialization—the common term used is *team work*. It is for this reason that team athletes are often regarded as bearers of peace on the international level and patriotic cooperation on the national level. Business corporations like to hire team players partly because they value their experience of working with other people in large organizations, of having learned to take orders and constructive criticism, and because of their apparent ability to work within highly competitive situations.

There are other less flattering interpretations of team play, though. Some critics feel that team athletes represent rote conformity to the established order. Others believe that team sports are nothing more than models of aggression mirroring either the viciousness of ruthless business tactics or the waging of international war itself. Team athletes often fight for positions that are allotted by a third party, usually a team *manager* or *coach*. In addition to competing with opponents, then, they must also fight their own teammates. Individual athletes compete solely with opponents and need no one's approval for their undertakings. As long as they win, they may keep advancing; and if they lose, no one complains to them. Team athletes, though, are only a part of a win or loss; and how much of a role they had in either is often a matter of interpretation, observation, persuasion, and bias.

Salaries are often a reflection of similar processes. Team players are offered payment according to how much they are thought to have contributed to their team's past victories or losses. An individual athlete either wins a prize, or does not. No one argues with him or her about salary or benefits. In effect, the team player is like the employee of a large company, while the individual player is more like the self-employed business owner.

For this reason there is often more direct pressure on individual athletes. They must perform well consistently in order to maintain their standing and livelihood. Team athletes, on the other hand, are guaranteed a stated salary, regardless of their daily performance during the life of their contracts. Team players in a slump can assume a less significant role on the team—or even accept a salary cut during the next contract negotiations. They also have countless opportunities to divert their careers into coaching, managing, or broadcasting. Individual athletes have fewer of these options readily available.

Managers and Recruiters

Managers, also called *head coaches*, are the direct leaders and supervisors of professional athletes. Generally speaking, managers and head coaches are employed by organizations that field a team of players to compete regularly in a specific sport. Since organized team play is a relatively new phenomenon in sports, so is the managing occupation. Before the professionalization of team sports in the 19th century, managing was virtually a nonexistent vocation.

Probably the earliest professional managers were the athletic head coaches of school sports. The British public schools (what are known in America as private schools) had hired *physical educators* since at least the early 19th century. Out of this tradition came the head football coaches of American college teams. Later, they were joined by head coaches and managers in other college sports—baseball, basketball, rugby, and soccer, to mention only some of the more popular ones. Although the players on these school teams were obviously amateurs, their coaches were paid professionals. They also often taught academic and physical education subjects in addition to their managing duties.

The job of manager became increasingly specialized and significant as team sports grew in popularity and complexity in the 20th century. Managers and head coaches today have very different duties than the coaches that are also under their supervision. While coaches are primarily responsible for building the skills and techniques of the players, the manager is responsible for motivating players to perform to the fullest of their potential for the good of the team. The manager or head coach must decide who will play, who will not, when a player ought to be taken out of a game, who will be the substitute, and so on. The managers's primary responsibility is to use the available players in such a way as to maximize the team's effectiveness.

The manager works closely with the team's owners in determining and interpreting policies that will affect the players and their performances. One of the most important of these joint responsibilities—also shared with *scouts* and *recruiters*—is the selection, recruitment, and release of player personnel. Scouts are hired primarily to learn advance information about opposing teams and players, in order to help their own team prepare for coming games. Recruiters are hired specifically to seek out and obtain high-quality players who will fit the needs of the team they represent.

Managers are generally given short-term contracts, which seldom exceed the length of one playing season. They are paid well compared with business managers and, of course, enjoy more visibility and esteem. They do not earn anything close to the salaries of the star players, however. This is often a point of tension in a ball club, especially since the lower-paid manager is responsible for assuming authority over all of the players, including the stars. When such problems become severe or too public, team owners are often faced with the difficult task of deciding who is more important to keep on the team—the star or his manager. Often, one must go.

Managers are usually chosen from the ranks of former players or coaches. Ironically, the best managers and head coaches have often been players who were only mediocre at best. Managers have longer careers than players. While the latter usually perform between the ages of 20 and 40, managers are rarely younger than 40. Therefore the two careers can be very conveniently combined. Since it is difficult to place precise blame on a failing team, however, and because there can be only one ultimate seasonal champion out of sports leagues of 20 or so teams, managers are frequently scapegoats. For this reason, managers are usually hired, fired, re-hired and re-fired with uncommon regularity.

Another type of managing, usually associated with professional *boxers*, is promotional managing. These managers act as both coaches and *promoters*. They arrange purses and fights for their clients and also coach them through training and into the ring. They are extremely well paid, usually earning about a third of the boxer's "take." Before the late 19th century, promotional managers rarely existed, as prizefighters usually arranged their own bouts and kept all of their profits.

Promoters of other sporting events earn a percentage of the house or gate receipts of a particular event. Before the 20th century, promoters were not professionals, but they did stand to gain from the arrangement of sporting events. In ancient Greece, local kings and merchants often aided the promotional work involved in the preparation for the Olympic Games. In ancient Rome, emperors and other public officials promoted gladiatorial and related events. Medieval lords and merchant guilds were instrumental in setting up tournaments and fairs that featured sports contests. All of these promoters had religious, political, or economic motivations, but the modern commercial promoter is guided strictly by economic considerations.

Sports Officials

Sports officials include *scorers* or *scorekeepers, timers, field judges, referees*, and *umpires*. Their job is to see that sports and games progress with as little confusion or interference as possible. To do this, they must be keenly aware of the rules, guidelines, boundaries, and codes of conduct related to the particular event that is being officiated.

In ancient Greece, officials were used to watch over physical contests such as *wrestling* and *pankration* (a type of boxing). They were usually armed with clubs to reprimand those who broke the rules. One of the great attractions of the Roman blood sports (for the audience) was the absence of officials to supervise them. The giver of the games—the sponsor—was the one who usually decided if any "rules" had been broken and, if so, what to do about it. Such questions as whether a defeated *gladiator* should be granted life or sentenced to death in the arena were left to the giver's discretion. For this, he often turned to the mob for their show of approval or disapproval for a certain decision, and he would then "officiate" accordingly.

In Rome officials were employed to see that the popular horse and chariot races—on which large sums were wagered—were run fairly and according to the ground rules of the track. Horse-racing *intermediates* were also commonly used in medieval times to record racing results and determine the winner in a close race. In the 17th century, when racing began to feature a list of six or seven rather than just two horses, horse-racing officials or "keepers of the match book" became more important and more commonly professional. Modern *bookmakers* are descended from these officials.

With the advent of organized sport in the 19th century, *officials* emerged as a fully professionalized group of workers. The complexity of games, the intricacy of their rules, the exactness of ground rules, and the importance of observing precisely what happened in an instant put severe demands on the performance of officials. The result has been a splintering of duties into many specializations.

In boxing, official *scorers* are now used to judge the winners of matches, while in other sports scorers determine statistical information such as whether or not a dropped fly ball in a baseball game should count as a hit for the batter or an error for the fielder. The function of the official scorer, then, varies from the most important job of judging world championships to details that in no way affect the outcome of the contest, like the evaluating of performances in baseball. They also, of course, keep an accurate record of the number of points actually earned during contests such as tennis and golf.

Timers have the important task of deciding whether or not a play counts as one that may be scored. This, of course, pertains only to timed sports such as football, basketball, and hockey. Such judgments may be critical, as in basketball when a basket counts for two points only if it left the shooter's hand before regulation time expired. If not, the basket does not count.

Judges, referees, and *umpires* are the on-the-field assessors of what is fair, what is not, what may be scored, and what may not. These are the officials who stay in the thick of the action and determine the consequences of every single play and its components.

Officials, especially *field judges*, are often the objects of player protest and spectator derision. They must be firm and resolute in their decisions so that the contest does not get out of hand. In the United States the judgments of field officials are almost always final. Instant replay television cameras sometimes prove that a judgment was made in error. In some sports, such as football, such evidence is sometimes taken into account and a decision changed. In other cases, however, that evidence does not alter or even figure in the decision, which is an immediate one. The common reasons given for this are that it would slow the game down and that two-dimensional electronic images are not always more accurate than the three-dimensional ones of real life. In many other parts of the world, notably Europe and Latin America, officials may give the advantage of a "close call" to the home team, because players and fans frequently react to unpopular decisions with mob violence. In the United States, players are immediately ejected from a contest if they physically contact an official in protest, and fans are never permitted on a playing field during regulation time. Officials are protected by strict security.

Field officials are often former players of the sport in which they now judge. In most cases they must be in excellent physical shape, since they need to run after the players to follow the play that they are to judge. Basketball, football, soccer, and rugby officials must be in particularly good condition.

Officials in most sports are trained for their profession in schools. Baseball umpires have particularly demanding requirements to meet, including usually long minor league internships before reaching the major leagues.

Job lists for prospective officials are relatively short, making the career highly demanding and competitive. Most officials today belong to labor unions, although they are often part of player associations, thus somewhat undermining their representative value. Many different groups of officials are now in the process of trying to form exclusive collective bargaining unions to serve their unique needs.

For related occupations in this volume, *Performers and Players*, see the following:
Actors
Dancers
Racers
Variety Performers

For related occupations in other volumes of the series, see the following:
in *Artists and Artisans*:
Painters
Sculptors
in *Communicators*:
Authors
Journalists and Broadcasters
in *Financiers and Traders*:
Merchants and Shopkeepers
in *Harvesters*:
Farmers
Fishers
Hunters

in *Healers* (forthcoming):
   Physicians and Surgeons
in *Helpers and Aides*:
   Bath Workers
in *Leaders and Lawyers*:
   Police Officers
in *Restaurateurs and Innkeepers* (forthcoming):
   Innkeepers
in *Scholars and Priests*:
   Priests
   Teachers
in *Scientists and Technologists*:
   Statisticians
in *Warriors and Adventurers*:
   Gamblers and Gamesters
   Soldiers

Dancers

For most of human history, dance, drama, and music have been closely intertwined. In the West *actors* and *dancers* separated 2,500 years ago, in Greece; but in most of the world, that separation never occurred. Throughout Africa, Asia, and Oceania, as well as in the pre-colonial cultures of the Americas, that close intertwining continues. In these areas the talents of actor-dancers are employed in a unified dance theater, which, in its native forms, has seen none of the separation between drama and dance so characteristic of the Western theater, first in Greece and then again since the Renaissance. However, the world is an ever-smaller place, especially since the advent of movies and television, so that in much of the world Western forms co-exist with native forms. Dance continues to be a major worldwide artistic form, and dancers continue to form one of the most substantial of artistic professions. That is as it has been for thousands of years.

Humans have danced since long before there were historical records. The cave paintings of southern Europe and southwestern Asia strongly suggest that dance—like drama—was one of the first organized human activities, and was an essential part of the earliest human rituals and religious observances. Dance and drama evolved together, but the available evidence indicates that the professional dancer emerged on the world stage long before Thespis, the first professional actor, appeared at the Athens Dionysia in 534 B.C.

Professional dancers appeared first as trained performers involved in religious rituals, employed by the religious or government organizations (often the two were combined) to whom they were attached. Such dancers often performed other functions in addition to dance, but over the course of many centuries, dancers in several cultures emerged as a separate group of highly skilled professionals.

As archaeological research illuminates human history, the history of the dance profession continues to lengthen. Sophisticated dances seem to have been performed by male and female dancers attached to Egyptian temples as early as 3000 B.C. By the 25th century B.C., a highly developed body of ritual dances performed by trained dancers was an essential part of Egyptian religion. During the same period, the Egyptian nobility began importing trained dancers as entertainers. The Egyptian king Neferikare, in the 25th century, wrote of a "pygmy of the dances of the god of the Land of the Spirits," who was being brought to his court; the reference implies the existence of a long dance tradition in a country outside Egypt, probably Ethiopia.

On the other side of the ancient world, in China, professional dancers may have been attached to the courts of the early Chinese emperors as early as 2500 B.C., and were native to northern India in the same period. The

Dancers like these at the Shinto Temple at Nara, Japan, have long been associated with religion. (From The New America and the Far East, *by G. Waldo Browne, 1901)*

evidence so far is relatively slight, but dancers were clearly working in China and India by about 1500 B.C., so professional development is thought to have begun considerably earlier.

Although Egyptian dance styles are far from clear, the dance seems to have been characterized by movement of the whole body as in later Western dance. In contrast, Indian dance—that great precursor of all classical south and east Asian dance forms—focused on movements of the upper body, arms, and head, with a relatively immobile trunk.

In the course of 3,000 years of development, Egypt trained religious dancers whose work focused on ritual expressions of religious beliefs, especially in funerary practices, but also in a variety of temple-connected festivals occurring throughout the year. Male *priests* were involved in dance ritual from the first, but the trained temple dancers seem to have been almost exclusively female.

By about 1500 B.C., secular professional dancers were also working in Egypt, primarily as entertainers of the nobility. They were by no means all Egyptians, for by then considerable commercial traffic and cultural exchange had developed among the Bronze Age cultures of Africa and Eurasia. Considerable evidence indicates that African and Indian professional secular dancers worked in Egypt in this period, often imported as slaves. During the last thousand years B.C., troupes of dancers were working as independent professionals in the larger Egyptian cities. By the time of the Roman conquest, the tradition of the Egyptian dance was old and well established in both religious and secular life. There is every reason to believe that contemporary Near Eastern civilizations, fully as developed as Egypt's in terms of religious and ritual forms, and similarly joining church and state as one, also possessed a body of trained religious dancers attached to courts and temples, as well as professional dancers for secular audiences.

Across the Mediterranean, probably influenced by Bronze Age Crete and perhaps Egypt as well, the Greeks developed professional dancers. The training of Greek male dancers was soon intertwined with the development of the Classic Greek theater. Although the early members of the Greek theater's chorus were amateurs, by the fourth century B.C. they were professionals. These chorus members—all male—were dancers and choral singers, moving in patterned forms on stage and providing much of the unity between music, dance, song, and story that characterized the Greek theater. These professionals were organized into guilds, and to some extent shared the high status held by *actors* in the Greek world.

The history of the dance is only partly joined with that of the theater, however, for women dancers were barred from the Greek stage. But—as in other cultures that excluded them from theater, including Elizabethan England and feudal Japan—women dancers continued to work. In Greece they worked as young dancing *mimes*, as private entertainers, as temple dancers, and as *dancer-prostitutes*, in Greece called *heterae*. In Greece, as in so many other cultures, the identification of female dancers with prostitution had profound adverse effects upon the social status of women dancers. That effect persisted strongly in much of the world for many centuries and to some extent continues today.

As Greece declined, the center of the Western world shifted to Rome. There both female and male dancers worked on the same stage, and with very few exceptions shared very low status, the vast majority being *slaves*. Roman drama, strongly influenced by the Greeks, flourished in the second and first centuries B.C. But by 29 B.C.—at the end of the 500-year-old Roman Republic and the beginning of what would be 500 years of the Roman Empire—the influence of the Greek theater had all but disappeared in Rome. By the early first century A.D., the major entertainment forms were those of the variety theater. It was a theater of dancers, mimes, *acrobats, jugglers, animal trainers*, and *athletes*—of huge city audiences and star performers. This fit into both the main Etruscan-Atellan theater tradition and the kind of society that evolved during the course of the Roman Empire.

But whatever the shortcomings of the Roman theater, and of the society it so well represented and served, it was also a theater that produced a major new Western form, that of the *dancer-mime* or *pantomimist*. In the theater of the empire, some pantomimists became great stars, the greatest of their time and place—and their place was Rome, the center of Western civilization. The first two stars of Roman pantomime were Pylades of Cicilia and Bathyllus of Alexandria. These two professional dancers and mimes are sometimes credited with having originated the form during the reign of Augustus, near the beginning of the Christian era.

Roman pantomimists worked on stage in masks, usually as soloists in elaborate costumes, wordlessly acting out story lines that had often been at least partly explained to their audiences by the *narrators* who introduced them. The pantomimists were dancers, accompanied by music; at first, by only a flute or flute and lyre, later by a group of instruments functioning as an orchestra. Many pantomimists were highly trained and skilled performers enjoying the same kind of celebrity and income accorded well-known performing artists in modern times.

Their art survived the spread of Christianity to Rome; their celebrity and income did not. After the establishment of Christianity as the Roman state religion in 393 A.D., Roman dancers, mimes, and pantomimists, along with all the other performers of the Roman variety theater, found themselves forced to the fringes of Roman life by the Christian Church, which from the first deeply opposed the theater professions.

Yet audiences remained, and professional dancers continued to work, some as dance teachers, as had been true since the days of the Roman Republic. Much later, in the sixth century A.D., after the fall of the Western Roman Empire, Theodora, a pantomimist of the Eastern Roman Empire, even became the wife of the Emperor Justinian. This in a sense underscored the durability and longevity of the form throughout the Mediterranean world. The popularity of pantomime and of its performers was to serve the dance theater well. It would survive many hundreds of years of Christian persecution in the West, to form much of the traditional and artistic basis for the *commedia dell'arte* theater troupes of Renaissance Europe.

Dancers in the East

Meanwhile dance continued to thrive in the East. Classical Asian dance remained closely tied to the temple and to the various state religions and court societies. In antiquity, the most famous of the early temple dancers were the *devadasi* of South India. These *temple girls* danced in service to Shiva (the god of Dance), who was thought to have created the whole universe through his dance—the Dance of Creation. They performed at many important ceremonies and during processions and rites. Their greatest reputation, though, was for their practice of prostitution, also performed in service to the god.

By the third century B.C. a Hindu book on the form and essence of religious music, drama, and dance appeared. The *Natya Shastra*, by Bharati, considered the three art forms as one. Indeed, dancers were not a specialized group at this time. They performed music (often using a drum or other percussion instrument) while they danced, and used similar gestures in both dramatic and danced performances. Gesture constituted the most distinctive feature of Eastern dance, in ancient times as well as today. Indian dancers were trained to perfect three areas: *natya*, or dramatic mimicry of gods and persons; *nritta*, or bodily movement to musical accompaniment; and *nritya*, combining both facial expression and gesture. The *nritta* and *nritya* were typical of the Asian style of working *with* gravity instead of against it. By contrast, the Western dancer often tries to overcome gravity—in ballet, for example, through point-work, elevation, and leaps. In Asia most movements and gestures were heavy and directed *toward* rather than away from the earth. They were also highly stylized. For instance, there were precisely 13 head gestures; 36 glances; 7 movements each of the chin, eyeballs, and eyebrows; 9 of the eyelids; and 6 movements each of the nose, cheeks, and lower lip. The hands were the most important of all; there were 67 *mudras* (hand gestures) that dancers spent many years perfecting.

The postures and gestures used in Hindu dance may seem stiff to Westerners. Indeed, the *Natya Sastra*, laying down the "principles of dramatic art," was derived from the graphic arts—sculpture and painting—rather than from the performing arts. This formal, heavily stylized form typified dance in Cambodia, Thailand, Burma, and Indonesia as well as India.

In the Far East, however, dance was more fluid and sensuous, owing largely to the absence of the austere Hindu influence. Dance in China, Japan, and Korea was still primarily religious and moralistic. But it was influenced more by the principles of Buddhism, Taoism,

Indian dancers, like this street performer in Bombay, developed their own particular art style. (From History of India, *by Fannie Roper Feudge, 1903)*

269

and Confucianism—religions that were far less formal than the Hinduism directed by the Brahmin priestly caste. It was in the imperial courts of China, Japan, and Korea that Asian dance first emerged as a serious art form by about 500 years A.D.

The first professional dancers in the Far East were probably those attached to these grand courts. By at least the seventh century A.D., Japanese dancers held high positions as *civil servants* of the state. In Korea, dancers were often dignitaries, *treasurers*, and *bureaucrats* as well as dancers. Their various duties to and positions in the state were carefully outlined. The greatest thrust of professionalism in dance in the East came from China, during the T'ang dynasty, from the seventh through the tenth centuries A.D. This was a period of generally high cultural achievement, making China the artistic center of the East. Dance became a major concern under T'ang emperor Hsüan Tsung, who in the eighth century dedicated the "Pear Garden" as a court-school of dance and other performing arts. Over a thousand students flocked to the school. Once they became accomplished dancers, they might find a spot on government payrolls as entertainers at banquets and ceremonies. Women and girls often served the emperor and other high court personnel directly, becoming a permanent part of their retinues, and frequently acting as private *concubines* as well.

Dancers in the West

Dance did not fare so well in the West. After the fall of the Western Roman Empire, dancers in the Eastern Roman Empire continued to work in the variety theater. But the art of the professional dancer survived only in the small troupes that took to the road and stayed there during much of the medieval period. The performing artists of these troupes were called *joculators, troubadours, minstrels,* and *minnesingers* at various times and in the several countries in which they worked. Many worked in several forms at once; they were trained as dancers, *singers, jugglers, acrobats*, and *instrumentalists*. These performing artists worked at festivals in the open air, often for the growing feudal nobility, as did the traveling troupe of entertainers in Shakespeare's *Hamlet*. They lived on the edge of subsistence, depending on each succeeding feudal lord for permission to perform in his domain. Only in much later times, during the Renaissance, did some begin to receive royal and noble patronage and protection. Dancing and the other performing arts were entirely apprenticeship occupations, which were often passed down through many successive generations.

In the late Middle Ages the development of social dancing among the feudal nobility created a new situation for some dancers in these traveling troupes. Once again, as had been true in Rome 1,500 years earlier, amateurs required instruction from professionals—amateurs who could pay in money, protection, and status. The *dancing masters* of the early Renaissance were drawn from among the medieval traveling dancers. But the Italian dancing masters were no longer the wandering, low-status strolling players of the Middle Ages. They were people of substance, mentors of the courtly dance. In the process of tutoring the nobility, they were creating an audience for the professional dance theater. And these were the professionals who would later develop the Renaissance dance theater—the ballet.

The earliest-known European Renaissance book on dance, *On the Art of Dancing and Directing Choruses*, was published in 1416. Written by Domenica da Piacenza, it was the first of what would ultimately be a flood of books on every aspect of the European dance. In it, da Piacenza began the process of formalizing the European dance theater, with detailed descriptions of the *balli* dances being created in that period by Italian dancing masters. Two of his many students also produced important works—Guglielmo Ebreo of Pesara, one of a substantial number of Jewish-Italian dancing masters, and Antonio Cornazano, who wrote *The Book of the Art of the Dance*.

By the late 15th century, the courtly dance of northern Italy was more and more a dance of spectacle. Elaborately costumed and formally organized, it was performed by thousands of eager amateurs drawn from the nobility but taught by professionals.

At the same time, many professional dancers continued to work in the open air, part of the troupes of entertainers who had been on the road since the fall of Rome. With the increasing commercial prosperity of the Renaissance and growing urban centers, festivals and fairs sprang up throughout Italy, especially in the prosperous North. These often generated huge pageants, involving both local populations and many traveling troupes. These professionals and the dancing masters provided the theater dancers of the next two centuries. These were the artists from whose polished skills developed the *commedia dell'arte* theater companies, the dancers of the *ballet*, and the artists of the *opera*.

Precursors to the ballet included the early *ballets de cour*, the court spectacles climaxing formal occasions, such as weddings and tournaments; the *intermezzi*, short dance-dramas accompanying banquets, in the early Renaissance increasingly focusing on mythological themes; and the *masquerades* favored in 16th-century England, in which masked players performed dance-dramas before the nobility. Though dance was popular throughout Europe, it was in France that professional dancers, many of them Italian, developed the main theater dance forms of the Renaissance and beyond.

Catherine de Medici of Florence, in the 16th century Queen and then Queen Mother of France, was the original patron of the ballet in France. She sponsored many pageants and spectacles, notably the *Ballet de Polonais* staged in 1573, a dance spectacle organized for the arrival of Polish ambassadors in France. It featured masked dancers performing exceedingly intricate courtly dance figures. Then in 1581, she sponsored the *Ballet Comique de la Reyne Louise*, widely regarded as the first true ballet, a massive spectacle uniting drama, dance, songs, and music, which played to an audience estimated at 10,000 persons. Costing the then-enormous sum of 3,600,000 francs, it was produced and directed by the Italian dancing master Baldassari de Belgiojoso, who had adopted the French name Balthasar de Beaujoyeuix. He had previously coached the dancers of the *Ballet de Polonais*.

In the latter part of the 16th century, the modern stage, with its proscenium arch, was developed in Italy. With the advent of many permanent theaters in Italy, France, England, and Spain during the next half century, theater dance increasingly became the province of professional dancers. Louis XIV of France danced for almost 50 years on the French ballet stage. He was known as the Sun King because of his appearance as the sun in the *Ballet de la Nuit* at the age of 15 in 1633. But in the 1630's professional dancers were dancing beside him, and by mid-century they were playing the leading roles. It was Louis XIV who hired the Florentine Giovanni Battista Lulli—in France called Jean-Baptiste Lully—as ballet *producer, director*, and sometimes performer. Pierre Beauchamps, whom some credit with establishment of ballet's five basic positions, was Louis's ballet master, or *teacher*. Louis established the Royal Academy of the Dance in 1661, which in 1669 was merged with the Royal Academy of Music, and ultimately became the Paris Opéra.

In the early days of the French ballet, many female roles were played by men, although women had long played in the French theater. By the latter 17th century, however, Lully was training both women and men at the Royal Academy, and in 1681, women began to appear in starring roles on the French ballet stage.

Like the other major French companies of the period, Lully's Academy of the Music and Dance, called the Opéra, was both government-subsidized and a sharing

In 17th-century France, nobility including the king himself, took part in the dances, this one on an American theme. (New York Public Library, Spencer Collection, c. 1662)

company, in which the dancers shared the profits of their productions. This was to remain true until the French Revolution. After 1789, subsidies were lost, but returned with Napoléon. And after the end of the 18th century, only the Comédie Française remained a sharing company. Performers in all other theaters, including those in ballet, were salaried employees in acting companies run by *actor-managers*.

The ballet theater began very early to be a theater of dominant performers, or *stars*. By the end of the 17th century, leading dancers were beginning to emerge. One of the first graduates of the Opéra ballet school, established in 1713, was Gaetano Vestris, the outstanding male star of his day. At the same time, a series of star *ballerinas* began to dominate the French ballet stage, starting with Marie-Anne Camargo and Marie Gallé. The star tradition became a permanent feature of the ballet theater, as of the Western theater as a whole.

In the 17th century, when professional dancers began to appear side by side with nobility on the French ballet stage, dancers worked in masks, in elaborate and often heavy costumes. The women were encumbered by corsets and high-heeled shoes, without the pointed toe so characteristic of modern ballet. The stages were full of scenery, and spectacular productions were moved by increasingly complex stage machinery. The productions in which dancers worked combined ballet and opera, including elements of spoken drama, singing, dance, and music. Molière and Lully collaborated on several works for the ballet theater, such as *Le Bourgeois Gentilhomme*, in modern times produced as plays without dance.

By the mid-18th century, professional dancers like Marie Gallé had taken over the ballet. (Engraving by N. Larmessin after a painting by Nicolas Lancret)

For the next three centuries, dancers worked in a theater that became first a European and then a worldwide dance theater. Its language has continued to be French and its dominant style—that of the "classical" ballet—has continued to be that of the French royal court of the 17th century, when the Sun King and Lully danced together. Yet although language and formal style seemed to change little, many changes occurred onstage. By the time of the French Revolution, the ballet was the province of the professional dancer. Although still subsidized by the state, the ballet was by the middle of the 18th century a popular form, and increasingly so throughout Europe. All during the 18th century, dancers became freer on stage, as costumes became lighter, heels disappeared from shoes, wigs and masks were discarded, men began to wear tights, and technique developed.

Throughout Europe, opera and ballet began to separate. In Italy, the opera became the dominant form, although dancers and *choreographers* of the Italian school had been foremost in the early decades of ballet. In France, ballet became the dominant native form. The English masques of the Stuarts became early ballets-without-words—called the *ballets d'action*—starting with John Weaver's *The Loves of Mars and Venus* in 1717. This was the main form that ballet was thereafter to take. But England did not develop a native ballet movement until the 20th century. French dancers and choreographers developed the *ballet d'action*, in accordance with the reforms advocated by the French dancer and choreographer Jean Georges Noverre in his *Letters on Ballet and Dancing* in 1760.

Modern Western Dancers

After the Napoleonic Wars, in a Europe entering the modern period and swept by Romanticism in the arts, the ballet became an extraordinarily popular form of mass entertainment. This was the ballet of the great star ballerinas, of Marie Taglioni and Fanny Elssler, who now danced on their toes, *en pointe*. Taglioni was the first star ballerina to do so, mastering the technique in 1832 in her role in *La Sylphide*. That ballet was choreographed by her father, Philip Taglioni, beginning a new period in the history of ballet. The great line of Italian dancers also continued in this period. Perhaps most influential of them was Carlo Blasis, whose *Elementary Treatise on the Theory and Practice of Dancing* and *Code of Terpsichore* provided a system of theory and practice for the ballet. The theory has to a considerable extent been replaced in the modern period, but the practice still provides the instructional basis for the ballet.

In the mid-19th century, the center of the ballet began to shift from France to Russia, although the ballet continued to expand as a medium of mass entertainment throughout the world. Russia had been hospitable to the ballet. Its rulers had established the Imperial School of the Ballet in 1740, reflecting Russia's rapid Westernization and strong ties to French culture. The royal family heavily subsidized the ballet, and many in the nobility emulated the royal family, sponsoring local ballet companies. The Moscow Ballet, which later became the Bolshoi Ballet, was formed in 1825. In 1837, Marie Taglioni danced *La Sylphide* in St. Petersburg to enormous acclaim.

The Russian ballet was a ballet of spectacle, using native as well as foreign themes. Its dancers worked in a social context much like that of the French court of the 17th century, but in the 19th-century mode. They became Europe's leading dancers during the years 1862 to 1910, after the French dancer and choreographer Marius Petipa, who had gone to Russia as a dancer in 1847, became assistant *ballet master* and choreographer of the Russian state ballet. In the next half century, he worked with Tchaikovsky and other Russian *composers* in the creation of scores of ballets, and with Christian Johannsson of the Imperial School of Ballet to develop a corps of dancers who were, in their time, the best in the world.

In the early 20th century, the Russian ballet—still the world's leading dance theater—was revitalized through the influence of impresario Serge Diaghilev, choreographer Michel Fokine, and a group of composers, the most prominent of whom was Igor Stravinsky, working with such dancers as Vaslav Nijinsky and Anna Pavlova. Diaghilev's Ballet Russe opened in Paris in 1909, and was an extraordinary success. Its example revolutionized Western ballet, especially after the Russian Revolution, when many people of the Russian ballet emigrated from Russia. These Russian dancers continued their lives and careers in many other countries, forming a new core for 20th-century ballet.

In the 20th century, ballet dancers—if they are successful—enjoy the same celebrity, income, and social status accorded other performing artists. As has been true for centuries in the dance, professional training starts early, roughly between the ages of eight and ten. The years of training are long and hard, the competition strong, and the working life short and insecure.

After the Russian Revolution, the focus of the world ballet theater moved westward, to Europe and the United States between the world wars, and then increasingly focused on New York and London after World War II. In many respects, such as dance styles and costumes, ballet was still fixed in the conventions of the past. Some dancers and choreographers, however, adapted very successfully to a new environment. For example, the Americans developed a far more "physical" style on stage than that of their European predecessors. And, like the Russians before them, the Americans began to weave their own themes into their repertoire. The classic Russian choreographer George Balanchine worked in Paris during the early part of the interwar period and emigrated to New York in 1933 to form the American Ballet Theater and its associated school. He provided a bridge between the classical European ballet and the new American ballet, training American dancers, working in both classical and American themes, costumes, and forms. In essence, Balanchine played the same role in the United States in the 20th century that Petipa had played in Russia in the previous century.

In the 20th century, the ballet, undisputedly the main serious Western dance-theater form since the Renaissance, began to share its eminence with, and to be influenced by, a new dance form—the *modern dance*. Originating in the United States, and now a worldwide dance movement, the modern dance is so far largely a dancer's theater, its choreographers often working with self-expressive, rather than narrative forms. It has developed in a period that has seen no counterparts to those classical composers who wrote for the ballet; in a sense, it has yet to meet its music.

The American dancer Isadora Duncan was the first leading exponent of the modern dance. Without formal training, she began to develop the modern dance as a concert-theater form toward the end of the 19th century. She first toured Europe in 1899, with great popular success and powerful impact upon the theater artists of her time. Her contribution was an idea and an early standard of performance; she founded no school, built no theater company, and left no body of work. Yet her ideas and style were so powerfully conveyed, and the time was so right, that she is properly described as the founder of the modern dance movement. It remained for others to found schools and develop that movement, notably Ruth St. Denis and Ted Shawn, later Martha Graham, and even later the great line of Black United States and Caribbean dancers and choreographers—Katherine Dunham, Pearl Primus, Alvin Ailey, and many others. All have created distinctive work, which merges with that of the earlier modern dancers to form what is now the modern dance.

Modern dancers move far more freely than do dancers in ballet. From Duncan on, men and women have reached for work that flows freely, the women dancing not on their toes, but in a new form that created in its dancers and choreographers a feeling of intense desire to achieve self-expression. Conventions develop in every artistic form, of course; the earliest great workers in every field set the forms followed by others later. But that has so far happened only to a limited extent in modern dance, which therefore remains the main experimental area for the dance today.

Eastern Dancers into Modern Times

Eastern dance continued to develop independently. As society became more cosmopolitan, Asian temple and palace dancers were replaced by more sensuous and even erotic dancers, who performed in the cities for a rising merchant and middle-class audience. In the ninth century, female *maharis* and male *gotipuas* created a sensational stir in the Indian city of Orissa.

In the late 16th century, a popular dance theater known as *Kabuki* was started in Kyoto, Japan. Founded by a prostitute named Okuni, this dance form was so erotic that by 1629 the government banned it—at least as performed by female dancers. They were promptly replaced by young boys, particularly the *onna gata* (female impersonators). These boys were specially selected for training in this field, and their position came to be one of honor and envy. Nonetheless, by 1653, the government insisted that only adult males could perform the Kabuki professionally. The arrival of women and young boys into the world of urban entertainment set a lasting precedent in the East, however. Eventually, the Kabuki became a more artistic and serious dance form, attracting increasingly skilled dancers.

Other types of professional dancers also regarded their occupations as artistic rather than bawdy or sensuous. The rise of Zen Buddhism led to the creation of the Japanese *Noh* dance-drama in the late 14th century. Noh dancers—all male—differed significantly from traditional Eastern dancers in that they aimed to create suggestions, rather than using stylized, formal expressions, even though every movement was prescribed. That is, through their dance, they sought to create poetic imagery rather than moral lessons. In time, Noh dancers came to receive great gifts of patronage from *shoguns* (military rulers) and the landed gentry. Even those of less repute and skill often found suitable employment as civil servants involved in state productions.

Some dance forms were actually derived from the oral tradition and retained close links to it; dancers in these forms were actors, *dramatists*, and *reciters* as well. The Korean *Keesaengs* and the Japanese *geisha girls* recited poetry as well as performed dances before elite, courtly audiences. They enjoyed an elevated social standing that put them significantly ahead of the concubines and prostitutes who had generally given the dance profession—especially the females—a seedy reputation. In truth, women were largely kept out of the profession in Japan, while in India, Korea, and China they were relegated to roles as prostitutes (concubines and temple dancers included) or *servant girls*.

The occupation and status of the professional dancer in Asia changed little over the centuries until just very recently. The Noh dancers, for instance, were highly accomplished as artists, but were looked down upon as scoundrels and beggars by society in general. This may have been partly because their occupations forced them into lives of wandering, in addition to the traditional link of dancing with prostitution and sensual entertainment. Lately, though, as Asian dancers have come to be more closely associated with their roles as artists, this stereotypical image has finally undergone revision. During the 1930's, for instance, the southwestern Indian temple dancers—the devadasi, who had since ancient times been regarded as nothing more than prostitutes—became recognized as honorable professionals. Today, members of even the most elite levels of Hindu society aspire to become temple dancers. In Communist China, the popularization of ballet has done much to bestow a grand image on the professional dancer. In more traditional cultures, where religious and folk themes remain the core of the dance form, dancers are still commonly amateurs, as they have been for thousands of years. Such is the case of the masked folk dancers of Java and Thailand, the elaborately costumed dancers of Ceylon (now called Sri Lanka), and the gyrating, whirling *devil dancers* of Tibet.

In the West

In the West professional dancers since the Renaissance have continued to work in far more than the ballet and modern dance. The heirs of the dancers, singers, and mimes of the European traveling companies have worked in the music halls of many countries, in variety, in vaudeville, and in the musical theater, which once again joins dance, voice, music, and drama, as did the French ballet theater before opera and ballet parted company. Western dancers in the musical theater of the 20th century are very highly and often formally trained, usually in modern dance rather than ballet techniques. But their performances often are more reminiscent of the highly disciplined work of the *corps de ballet* than that of Isadora Duncan. They work in a dance theater far more varied than any that has previously existed. Dancers may work in ballet or modern dance; before a live audience of tens of thousands at a circus or before a crowd at a football game, much as in Greece or Rome; in a live musical; or in movies or television for an audience of tens of millions.

Dancers may also teach, whether at a formally organized and certified educational institution or rather informally, whether to potential professionals or to amateurs, who want to learn a few social dances. For the urge to dance is old and continues to be strong, and one of the main means by which dancers support themselves

Among the legion of dancers are the ever-popular chorus line. (From Gems From Judge)

is by teaching. That is as it was in Rome, and as it has been throughout history in the West, since the advent of the dancing masters of the early Renaissance.

For related occupations in this volume, *Performers and Players*, see the following:

Actors
Athletes
Musicians
Variety Performers

For related occupations in other volumes of the series, see
the following:
in *Helpers and Aides*:
    Servants and Other Domestic Laborers
    Undertakers
in *Leaders and Lawyers*:
    Political Leaders
in *Restaurateurs and Innkeepers* (forthcoming):
    Prostitutes
in *Scholars and Priests*:
    Priests

Directors

The directing function in the performing arts is as old as the arts themselves. *Directors* shape works destined for performance, in essence assuming responsibility for the final form of the produced work. Some type of directing has been necessary wherever performances have been put on—whether Mesopotamian pageants, Egyptian religious rituals, Chinese and Indian court dance performances, Greek dramas, Roman circuses, medieval morality plays, ballets, operas, puppet theaters, or modern stage productions.

Directing has often been combined with acting and managing. Actor-managed troupes have been a standard form of organization in the theater throughout the world until the early 20th century. The director as a distinct professional in the performing arts—except for the *producer-director* of complex spectacles—is a relatively recent creation of the Western theater. The directing and producing functions performed by *actor-managers, ballet masters, choreographers, conductors,* and *ringmasters* stretch far back in history.

In the dance, the directing role of the choreographer is clear. The choreographer, in essence, creates the dance as it will be performed by the company, specifying all that is to happen on stage, and working with music, design, and dance elements to create a finished job. In the course of doing so, the choreographer works with *dancers, conductors, designers, backstage crew, costumers*—all who have anything to do with the development of the finished work. Whether the choreographer works autocratically or democratically, the direction and production of the finished work are in the choreographer's hands. We have no evidence, but can guess that in the dance the choreographer's directing role goes very far back into human history. The Indian *Natya Sastra*, dating back in fully written form about 2,000 years and probably existing in part long before that, is nothing less than a detailed set of instructions covering every aspect of classical Indian dance-drama—a director's tool as much as a set of instructions to *actor-dancers*. The conductor performs the same function with the modern orchestra, having full responsibility for the finished work.

In the theater, too, we can see directors at work considerably earlier than the modern era, even though it is only in the last hundred years that the separate profession of theater director has clearly emerged. The European religious theater of the 14th through 16th centuries was a theater of pageant and spectacle, sometimes employing hundreds of people working together on the same stage, with many more doing supporting technical work. The nature of the work required the presence of a skilled coordinator, one who could take charge of the production from beginning to end, including every aspect of the work performed by those on stage. That was especially true because most medieval actors in religious drama were amateurs until very late in the development of that form. These were not the superb professionals of the *commedia dell'arte*, with hundreds of years of theatrical tradition behind them, and therefore able to move in ensemble on stage in fluid, rapidly forming, and re-forming patterns. These were the tradespeople of the towns, who needed precise instructions as to how, where, and when to move on stage. Such instructions ultimately became the responsibility of a single coordinating intelligence—that of the medieval director. Directors such as the Frenchman Jean Bouchet and the Spanish actor-director Lope de Rueda developed many religious dramas, often moving from place to place and repeating engagements year after year.

One extremely significant precursor of the modern theater director was the German *writer* and *dramatist*, Johann Wolfgang von Goethe. He became manager of the Weimar Theater in 1791, and active director-manager from 1796 through 1805, the year his dramatist-collaborator, Friedrich Schiller, died. In those years, Goethe was a director in the most autocratic of modern manners. He prepared each work in every detail, and worked with actors, designers, and crew to create a rigidly disciplined ensemble company. Goethe was scarcely a model followed by most theater directors in the 19th and 20th centuries; he was in all senses a choreographer of the theater. But his insistence on developing a company and a body of work reflecting his own unique views anticipated by almost a century a major modern image of the director as *auteur* (author). This image of the director's role today is encountered far more often among directors in screen forms than in the live theater.

Although Goethe's work represents, in practice, the earliest modern substantial unification of all elements of a theatrical production, it was three-quarters of a century before a body of theory and practice would develop that would lead to the emergence of the director as a major force in the theater. This appeared in the work of two people: Richard Wagner, whose theory of the unity of all theatrical elements was worked out in operatic production, notably from the time of the opening of his Bayreuth Theatre in 1876; and Georg II, Duke of Saxe-Meiningen, whose tightly disciplined troupe made an enormous impact on the theater of its day, touring for 16 years all over Europe, starting in Germany in 1874. The Meiningen troupe operated much as Goethe's Weimar troupe had done. But by then change was in the air, with a body of theoreticians and practical innovators ready to accept the concept of theatrical production as a unified artistic whole, with the director as prime mover. This was to become the major movement in the continental European theater of the 20th century.

The English-speaking theater did not follow suit. In England and America, the theater director never achieved the unquestioned dominance of such European figures as Jacques Copeau, Konstantin Stanislavsky, Vsevelod Meyerhold, Max Reinhardt, and later Bertolt Brecht and Jean-Louis Barrault. In film it was so, but not in the theater.

Gordon Craig, son of the English actress Ellen Terry, was the leading theoretician of the new director's theater. Although his work coincided with that of the Swiss musician and designer Adolphe Appia, it was Craig who exerted the most profound influence on the thinking of those developing the director's theater. Appia's early works expressed the concept of artistic unity as applied to the staging of musical dramas; Craig's work addressed itself to the spoken drama.

Craig's practical work was that of a designer for the stage. In this capacity he worked all over Europe during the first quarter of the 20th century. His most notable work was the design and direction of *Hamlet* at Stanislavsky's Art Theatre in 1912. But it was his written work—which called for the development of a single, unified art work in each production, with primacy of artistic creation assigned to the director—that caused a great storm of controversy in his time and provided the theoretical basis for the director's theater of the 20th century. His *The Art of the Theatre* was published in 1905, *Toward a New Theatre* in 1913, and *The Theatre Advancing* in 1919.

The emerging modern directors worked in no single style. A director might "choreograph" a work, as did Goethe or Meiningen, but might also come to work with little more than an idea, building the work as a unified whole in the course of rehearsal, as did Stanislavsky late in his career. What became common was not a single style, but the idea of the primacy of the director's role in creating the theatrical work. The dramatist's script, players, music, dance, scenery, costumes, lighting, and every other element of theatrical production were all seen as parts—but only parts—of that unified whole.

It is in screen forms that the modern director has achieved the most prominence. The mid-century concept of *auteur*—seeing the director quite literally as "author" of the completed film—is not dissimilar to Craig's view of the role of the director in theater, or for that matter Goethe's a century and a half earlier. The nature of film-making accentuates the importance of the director. In fact, for everyone else involved in a film, the work is a series of relatively disconnected acts. Even in those rare instances in which a film is shot in the sequence provided by its narrative line, the actors have no opportunity to develop sustained performances; they shoot the same bit again and again, with much of what is shot destined ultimately for the cutting-room floor. The nature of the medium makes it possible for the director to work with a single view, to create a unified work, without fully sharing that view or any element of control with the other artists involved in the production. Although movie and television stars are sometimes worldwide celebrities, in artistic terms films are uniquely the products of their directors. That has been true since soon after the advent of the medium. Although the early years of the century saw the filming of many works exactly as created for the theater, directors were soon using the new form in far more imaginative ways.

Italian film directors, such as Giovanni Pastrone and Enrico Guazzoni, were soon using the new form to once again create spectacle built around the Italian mime, in such works as Pastrone's 1913 film *Cabiria*. In Germany, the early screenings of Max Reinhardt's stage works soon were supplanted by the work of the German cinema's golden age—the silent films of such directors as Fritz Lang, Georg Pabst, and Ernst Lubitsch, many of whom immigrated to America after the rise of Nazism. The great Russian theater director, Vsevelod Meyerhold, who made only two films (both in 1915 and both now lost), became the teacher of a new generation of directors working in cinema, including Sergei Eisenstein. The French cinema enjoyed the extraordinary early work of Abel

The film director is sometimes dwarfed by massive sets, as this model of Tokyo Bay, and thousands of extras. (National Archives, Records of the Office of War Information, 208-AA-110N-1, c. 1943)

Gance, such as *Napoléon*. In the United States, soon to become the center of the world's cinema industry, directors D. W. Griffith, Thomas Ince, and Mack Sennett were by 1912 beginning to produce feature films, such as Griffith's landmark *Birth of a Nation*, in 1915.

Today's theater and film directors work in a worldwide director's theater almost a century old. Many are actors who have moved into directing, but an increasing number are formally trained only as directors. These often follow a sequence that includes academic specialization, apprenticeship, and career development solely in the director's occupation. In the live theater their degree of control and styles of work differ considerably from country to country. The director of a German repertory company is quite likely to assume considerably more control that the director of an American company assembled to present a single play. In the cinema, the director's primacy is unquestioned.

The director's work carries with it varying amounts of artistic prestige, depending largely upon the forms and national traditions in which a director works. In cinema, the director is supreme, a celebrity within the arts of no less stature than that accorded to star performers. Akira Kurosawa in Japan, Satyajit Ray in India, François Truffaut in France, and Francis Ford Coppola in the United States have all been accorded the same kind of worldwide artistic eminence. That kind of eminence has also been enjoyed by some choreographers and artistic directors such as ballet's George Balanchine, or conductors such as Arturo Toscanini. But among directors in the live theater, that kind of celebrity is far less often encountered in the modern period, and among television directors it is encountered very rarely, if ever.

For related occupations in this volume, *Performers and Players*, see the following:

Actors
Dancers

Musicians
Variety Performers

For related occupations in other volumes of the series, see
the following:
in *Communicators*:
Authors
Journalists and Broadcasters

Musicians

Professional *musicians* seem to have first appeared in the great civilizations of antiquity. For the most part, they were *composers*, *singers*, and *instrumentalists* all at once. Many were also *dancers* and *acrobats*, thereby affording a full range of entertainment and spectacle. There were musician social castes in early Mesopotamia, Egypt, and Judea. The occupation was frequently an inherited one. Being a professional musician or singer—usually both in these early times—offered uncommon comforts in a world where manual field labor, rugged housekeeping, and fighting were the chief occupations. Musicians were typically employed within the highest levels of society, enjoying many of the niceties of court and temple life. They took an active part in many of the great events of government and religion—royal ceremonies, coronations, and religious rituals and processions—as well as the festivities of ancient life, such as religious ceremonies, victory celebrations, and fertility rites. Their presence was also an essential ingredient of more somber occasions, such as funerals and death processions. *Army musicians* had important functions, such as directing march cadences and sounding communications and orders. Trumpets, drums, and tambourines were the chief instruments used by this group.

Although musicians lived comparatively easy lives, their work was not recognized as being very honorable or accomplished. Vast numbers of musicians retained in court and temple were *slaves*, often granted as gifts or tribute from foreign peoples, or taken as booty during war. Their songs and stories, dances and drama, however, played an important part in the transmission of cultural customs, ideas, and morals. Women musicians, particularly those taken as slaves, were frequently used also as *acrobats*, erotic *dancers, concubines*, and *prostitutes*. Despite this frequent exploitation of female musicians, many gained notable reputations as singers, dancers, and instrumentalists. Indeed, music was one of

Harpers like this one from a tomb at Thebes are widely represented in Egyptian art. (From History of Egypt, *by Clara Erskine Clement, 1903)*

the few fields that women could freely enter, particularly before marriage (after which they would usually be expected to turn their attentions strictly to homemaking).

While most musicians were part of official court and temple orchestras and choruses, some were freelance entertainers who found work at weddings and banquets in noble households, or who merely set up operations in the streets during festivals. These singers and instrumentalists, both men and women, most commonly worked in teams that also included *jugglers, acrobats*, and *dancers*. They might or might not be paid for their efforts. If so, their payment might well be in food or clothing. Some worked alongside *priests* and other *healers*, contributing strong rhythms that were thought to help in conjuring up spirits or easing the pain of childbirth. Because of its strong emotional character, music was employed liberally by amateurs in the healing and religious professions. Many priests and physicians learned music to use as part of their healing therapy, if they did not call for the assistance of professional musicians.

While early musicians may not have commanded great respect, they were appreciated for offering a soothing, if temporary, relief from the harshness of life. One Egyptian poet recognized the significance of the musician in this vein: "Call no halt to music and the dance, for soon your turn will come to journey to the land of silence."

Greek and Roman Musicians

Music progressed considerably during Classical times, particularly in Greece. Homer, Pindar, and other great poets and lyricists created a musical-poetical "literature" transmitted orally in a time when few people could read or write. They used a well-orchestrated mixture of music, song, dance, and mime to convey stories of the great achievements of *warriors, athletes*, and *princes*. Their epic poetry was spoken, but in a songlike rhythm that could almost hypnotize an audience. Music became an important feature of Greek culture, and eventually a standard part of the education of youth. Even athletic events were accompanied by the music of the lyre, plucked by the musician employed by the gymnasium.

For all the interest that the Greeks had in music, there were really very few professional musicians. The *harpmaster*, in charge of instruments, was a professional *teacher* of music more than an actual performer. The standard ideal in Greek life was for people to master most important things for themselves, making professionalism unwanted and highly suspect. Accordingly, each household had its own amateur musicians—usually the father or sons—who provided entertainment. The Greek refinement of music remained academic and strongly tied to various schools of philosophy, which had innovative ideas of music theory. The Pythagoreans, in particular, saw the harmony of music as one of the fundamental truths of the universe—one that they explored in great detail, to the definite betterment of the art. Still, *philosophers* were rarely accomplished or professional musicians, but rather theorists and academicians.

There were essentially three opportunities for aspiring Greek musicians. The most obvious was to win the patronage of the court or temple, serving as a private musician for a highly select audience, or for specific occasions and ceremonies. Such a life could be very leisurely and rewarding, but—as with all such situations in literature and the arts—it was highly competitive. For a long time, the great athletic contests, such as the Olympics, and regular festivals offered the greatest hope for accomplishment and reward in the field. While much has been written about the Greeks' love of athletic contests, they were almost equally fond of musical competitions. Grand prizes were awarded to those who performed well, with the most valuable ones generally going to those who sang while playing the *lyre*. Players of the *flute* and the *aulos* (both small wind instruments), and of the stringed *lyre* and *cithara*, won the next highest awards, followed by *choral* and *solo vocalists*.

Perhaps the greatest opportunity for steady, if not truly lucrative, employment was working for and performing with theatrical productions. Stage drama and comedy were renowned features of Greek culture, and music formed an essential aspect of their productions. Greek *choruses* presented a main portion of the dialogue as well as the background and commentary of a play. They sang lyrics that were well understood by the audience, and that added materially to the production. Choral singers enjoyed a fairly comfortable social status, for choral poetry was deeply ingrained in Greek tradition, dating back to the time of the Homeric epic *poets* and *lyricists*. They were instructed and directed by the master of the chorus—the *corrphaeus*—whose importance was second only to that of the *playwright* in the unique development of Greek drama and theater. Of course, playwrights themselves were often the lyricists and composers of what we would now call the musical "score"—to the Greeks a basic part of the play.

Greek choruses were, for the most part, made up of amateur singers. They performed not only for the theater, but also in cult rituals and processions at marriages, funerals, and celebrations. They were accompanied by both professional and amateur instrumentalists, chief of whom was the highly respected professional *aulete* (player of the aulos). The music of the theater, though, was sharply criticized by many observers, who felt that its loose style and rhythmic freedom was a drastic break with the sincere, moralistic, and monotonal character that had distinguished the professional *bards* and *songsters* of old. They noted that music had become so vulgar that even common wine parties were frequently spiced by the sounds of the freelance *aulos-girl*. By the end of the fifth century B.C., earthy instrumental improvisation had become so popular that it outstripped the efforts of the time-honored vocalist. Aristoxerus, a century later, was heard to complain that few musicians had even the slightest knowledge of the classics.

Professional musicians grew in numbers and organization. There was even a guild of *Dionysian artists*, singers and instrumentalists who performed within that particular cult. Music had become highly popular, but musicians were roundly despised by many for their lack of creativity and talent, and for their outrageous performance and instructional fees.

Under Rome, the status of musicians changed considerably over time. Well before the time of the Roman Republic, the *tibicines* (players of the *tibia*, a bone pipe) had enjoyed an enormously elevated status in Roman and probably Etruscan society. Plutarch noted that theirs was one of the oldest professional organizations in Rome. Tibia players performed magical tunes at ceremonial rites such as funerals, weddings, sacrifices, and offerings, and supposedly kept evil spirits away while attracting the gods. The lyre was almost as sacred as the tibia bone pipe, and the lyre players (*fidicines*) frequently accompanied the *tibicines*. But it was the latter who held a truly exalted social position, enjoying state privileges. They were even honored for the legendary labor strike of their guild in 311 B.C.

In the days after the Roman Republic gave way to the Roman Empire, though, the fortunes and prestige of the musical professions plummeted. Only the lowest class of individuals would aspire to enter this humble occupation. A great many of the *street singers* and even theatrical actor-musicians *(histriones)* were *slaves*. The general feeling was that the musician was a worthless vagabond who was either too degenerate or too simple to find a more respectable station in life. Many Romans also believed that the Greeks' love of music was an effeminate obsession. According to this criticism, music—like all the other arts, including athletics—had weakened the Greeks and contributed to their downfall. Certainly, no self-respecting freeborn Roman—no matter how desperate—would sing or dance or play instruments as an occupation, or even as a pastime for that matter. The only musicians who were tolerated were the resident Greeks and slaves, since it was no disgrace for them, and they could hope to do little better than that anyway.

The only type of music that the practical Romans really appreciated was the military music of the gallant field campaigns, announced by the colorful *trumpeters* and *horn players*—originally slaves, but later *soldiers* themselves, usually noncommissioned officers. The military musicians had an important function in the Roman army. Using a standardized series of signals, they gave notice of such events as camp breaks, attacks, retreats, and changes of guard—and even tipped off more subtle directions in strategic field maneuvers. In battle they often inspired the Romans while distracting the enemy. (This latter function may be somewhat similar to that of today's football-game band players, who try to help keep their team inspired and playing hard.) Besides this, they accompanied funerals, victory celebrations, and marches. So powerful were the military musicians that they even formed a sort of a mutual protection and compensation guild early in the third century A.D.

In time, musicians became somewhat more accepted in Roman society, and even some of the emperors were known to have courted music and its performers. There were still critics who did not approve of such activities, though. One contemporary of the Emperor Nero lamented that so distinguished an individual as the emperor himself could engage in "degrading efforts at singing with a *cithara* after the fashion of the stage." Still, music had gained popularity, especially in relation to the theater and in performance at the *circuses* and *games*. Some of the foreign *pantomimes* and *mimes*, who combined dancing and singing, had been quite a hit with the Roman public for several centuries. Whatever modest level of acceptance professional musicians received, however, even the best of them remained associated with the lowly dregs and scoundrels of the Roman street and tavern scene; their legacy is best summarized by their common label as the *infami*.

Eastern Musicians

In the East, musicians were regular members of court households. As early as the second century B.C., Chinese princes retained jugglers, small bell-and-drum orchestras, and singers, who not only entertained the elites, but also passed on a rich oral "literature." These were generally slaves, who had been trained for the purpose. Music was important in China from very early times. The imperial government even established an Office of Music which was charged with collecting music

Eastern musicians have often made heavy use of percussion instruments, as in this Burmese band. (From Peoples of the World, *19th century)*

and songs—especially those from Central Asia, which were especially popular—until the office was closed down in 7 B.C. Musicians, singers, and *variety performers* entertained the general populace, sometimes from special show-carts that rode through the towns. The best of the musicians, however, may have been the *priests* and *monks* who made a studied effort to make music, most typically the chant, an important part of their spiritual lives. Although many of these devoted musician-priests became highly accomplished and articulate in their own right, they cannot be considered professional musicians.

The eighth-century A.D. emperor Hsüan Tsung and his successors were especially fond of music. He founded the famous Pear Garden, in which hundreds of common-birth musicians and dancers—mostly young *court girls*—were trained, frequently under his personal direction. Many of these girls had been received at court as tributes and captives from foreign leaders, and often they had already been trained in the art of singing or playing instruments. The girls entertained dignitaries and visitors at court with gentle songs. They might also serve dinner to such guests, and offer them the comforts of bathing and massage. They were not unlike Japanese *geisha girls* of a later period.

Those who made serious occupations out of music were generally drawn from among the common people. During the medieval T'ang dynasty, singing *tavern girls* became popular in the meaner districts of the larger Chinese towns. Known as the *Chi Kuan* (*gishang* in Korea), they entertained with more than song and dance at the rowdy teahouses and brothels—places considered unfit for decent women, or upstanding men. Special amusement districts were eventually created in the main cities. Musicians and *actors* were to perform only there, so their licentious activities could be closely monitored by city authorities.

As urban life became more refined, musicians began to develop a distinct form of Chinese musical theater that gained rapidly in popularity, even with middle-class bureaucrats. (Much later, these productions evolved into the famous Peking Opera, which has emerged as the most important Chinese art form in modern times.) Musicians—both singers and instrumentalists—were also extremely important at sacred or social occasions. Whenever there was a procession—whether to usher in spring, to honor the dead, or to celebrate a wedding—musicians made part of the throng, sometimes playing alone, but equally often accompanying actors, jugglers, acrobats, and other performers.

Indian music was much less formalized. In very early Vedic times, the music seems to have been largely religious, of a simple chanting style, much like that found later in medieval Europe. Later secular music generally centered on lute-like instruments, on which the musician improvised multiple variations on known melodies. Music was for many centuries considered a genteel pursuit for the upper classes. An old Indian proverb runs: "The man who knows nothing of literature, music or art is nothing but a beast without the beast's tail and horns." By late medieval times, however, music had gradually become the province of lower-class professionals, who were eagerly sought by the upper classes.

Indian music had considerable influence on Chinese music, especially in the T'ang dynasty, and as a result on Japanese music, as well as that of the rest of Southeast Asia. In turn, it was somewhat influenced by the lesser Islamic tradition, notably in making bowed instruments important in Indian music. The voice was also treated as a musical instrument, and singers would improvise wordless variations on melodies, as if they were instrumentalists.

Medieval Musicians

In the West, as the Roman Empire fell into disarray, the professions of musicians and singers underwent considerable changes. In the early Middle Ages, the music professions became somewhat more secularized. Churches and cults were still the chief employers of musicians, particularly in the Eastern Roman Empire centered on Constantinople (Byzantium, today Istanbul). Yet there was some intrusion of professional singers and musicians, who were gaining acceptance in society. The mimes (*mimi*) of the Roman theater had long been despised (as the *infami*) for their common occupations; but they now appeared in the courts of barbarian kings. Attila the Hun retained many mimes and singers for his regular banquets. The Celtic *bards* of the British Isles gained prominence in court society, as did their counterparts, the *scop* in western and southern Europe, and the *skald* in northern Europe.

There was a great difference in the occupations of the bard and the mime. Bards were poets, historians, and ambassadors. The *skalds* of Norway and Sweden were regarded as extremely wise persons, many of whom served as intimate royal advisors. Bards frequently held high official positions at court and seem to have been generously rewarded. At a time long before mass media, such as newspapers or television, the bard's stories, reports, and intellectual presentations and monologues were eagerly sought by aristocrats and courtiers. Bards sang of deeds of valor, of politics, of war, and love. To some extent their messages provided propaganda for their patrons, as did the works of most pre-modern artists and writers. They typically provided accompaniment for their poetry, using a bowed, six-stringed instrument called a *crwth*, and were highly regarded as in-strumentalists as much as poets and intellectuals.

Mimes never achieved the stature of bards. Like their Roman predecessors, they remained on the fringe of society, entertaining in a variety of ways—some musical, some not, some so vulgar that church and state authorities joined forces in trying to limit their activities. Many mimes were women, who sang, danced, and offered post-show services of a more personal nature. Others were common stage actors, who enjoyed no greater repute. The mimes were *acrobats, singers, dancers, magicians, cardsharks, flame-* and *knife-eaters,* and *sideshow specialists.* Only occasionally did they display any talent as instrumentalists. They performed primarily for the lower classes, frequently for little more reward than a meal or a place to sleep for the night. Sometimes they gained favor within barbarian courts or (in the case of women mimes) were taken into royal harems. The influence of the church was so dominating a factor in the early Middle Ages, though, that mimes were never permitted to emerge from the shadows of their forebearers—the lowly, wretched, and despised *infami.*

The cultural influence of the Roman Catholic Church not only suppressed the activities of the mimes, but also forged a position of dominance in medieval music for the church itself. The church was the central agency of cultural and artistic developments in the early Middle Ages. In fact, it was chiefly in the monastery and in the liturgical pronouncement and refinement of what came to be called *plainsong* that the distinctive type of Western music as we know it survived at all. The term *plainsong* is actually a later term referring to the distinctive style of the *Gregorian chant*—the monophonic (single melody line) religious chant of the Catholic Church. Plainsong was both nonharmonic and monophonic, yet dramatically rhythmic. It was sung during Mass without instrumental accompaniment partly by the chorus (*schola*) and partly by the *cantor* (soloist). (In the Jewish temple ceremonies, the cantor was called the *chazzan.*) Because plainsong was one of the most important forms of devotion and spirituality, all clerics were obliged to take part in it. It was arranged monophonically to induce but never overbear contemplation, never to become itself the subject of devotion, but only the vehicle of it.

Even so, some priests became interested not only in modestly singing their parts in the chant, but in the whole spectrum of musical arts. It was these musical pioneers who eventually led the plainsong (and Western music itself) from its exclusively monophonic composi-

tion—with its single melody line—to a polyphonic enrich-
ment, in which two or more melodic lines create a
harmony. They developed the *organum*, which livened
the tone of plainsong by adding to the main part (the *vox
principalis*) one or more parallel voices (the *vox
organalis*). They also varied and expanded its melodic
base by improvising new words and music through the
technique called *troping*. These refinements, occurring
between the ninth and 12th centuries A.D., finally led to
the first truly polyphonic type of arrangement—the
motet. This added a full text to the upper part of the
chant, which continued to be delivered by a *cantus firmus*
tenor. The addition of such texts—both vocal and musical—led to a polyphony that gradually became more and
more embellished until the underlying plainsong was
hardly recognizable.

Secular Musicians

As great as its contributions were to music during both
the early and later Middle Ages, the clergy hardly
represented a musical profession. But many clerical
students who decided against becoming priests
benefited from their musical training and went on to
music-related occupations. The *goliards* were of this
genre. They were the first musicians drawn from the
middle class of society, but as a rule chose their
occupations in defiance of the values of their class and, in
particular, of the church hierarchy. Although they are
mentioned as early as the seventh century A.D., the height
of their activity came between the 10th and 13th
centuries.

At a time when most music was spiritual and devotional, goliardic songs stressed themes such as romantic
love, drinking, and gaming. Often obscene and typically
satirical of Christian morality, these song-poems were,
nonetheless, directed at middle- and upper-class
audiences, with whom the wandering goliards held an

ongoing intellectual debate. The song-poems were written in Latin and used monophony almost exclusively, so they did not really go beyond plainsong in terms of technical music accomplishment. The goliards were significant, though, in that they were essentially original *lyricists*. This was in contrast to most of the bards, who sang traditional songs, perhaps improvising at times, but seldom creating their own lyrics altogether. (One notable exception was the Norwegian convention of crediting the author and the reciter of songs separately—anticipating modern copyright laws.)

More popular and colorful than the goliards were the *mimes* of later medieval times. By the ninth or 10th century, they came to be known by other names—*jongleurs* (jugglers), in German *Gauklers*, in English *gleemen*, in French *joglars*. This breed of entertainers, singers, and musicians became much better accepted than the mimes of old. Many were excellent singers, dancers, and instrumentalists, and most combined these standard talents with bold showmanship and a variety of acts that included juggling, acrobatics, magic shows, feats of daring, trained-animal stunts, and the like.

The jongleurs traveled extensively from town to town and castle to castle in search of an audience or a patron. They did not write their own songs, as the goliards did, but were typically hired by court poets and aristocratic *troubadors* to sing and perform their compositions. Some were hired to entertain at weddings and noble banquets; others even went to live in aristocratic households. Many of the jongleurs were highly skilled singers and musicians, and by and large had a great deal more musical talent than the more-heralded troubadors. They sang in the vernacular (the spoken language of the people), rather than in Latin, and therefore became better known to the general public than either the goliards or the troubadors.

By the 14th century a higher class of jongleurs had emerged. Called *ménestriers*, they were socially acceptable and professionally elite. Although they still did not rival the troubadors in prestige, they far outnumbered them and eventually organized themselves into professional trade guilds named the *ménestrandise*. The ménestriers, like the goliards and jongleurs, were traveling entertainers; but unlike their compatriots, they received generally favorable acclaim

Wandering minstrels like this one played an important social role in medieval Europe. (From Illustrated London News, *19th century)*

that gave them the opportunity to perform before middle-class audiences. They came to fairly well monopolize that particular audience, especially as the goliards gradually abandoned their wandering musical ways and became students and *scholars* in the universities that began to be established in Paris, Bologna, and elsewhere during the Renaissance. In time, the ménestriers, the gleemen, the jongleurs, and the Gauklers came to be generally known as *minstrels*. While their professional strength was advanced considerably by their organization into guilds and fraternities, their initial success was in carrying forth the love songs of the troubadors.

Guilhem of Poitiers is thought to have been the first of the Provençal *troubadors*, apparently so-called because they were improvisers, or *tropers*. Later the word *tropers* was transformed to *tropators* and then to *trobadors*. As a court poet, Guilhem and others set several important precedents that would soon spread throughout Provençal and all of southern France. Surprisingly, Guilhem was a nobleman—the seventh count of Poitiers. Before his time, in the early 12th century, musicians were almost exclusively drawn from the common folk. The troubadors not only represented the first musicians from the privileged classes, but they even did their work in the vernacular, so their songs truly were "the first great flowering of secular art." This art soon spread to the north of France, where these poet-composers were known as *trouvères*, and to Germany where they were called the *minnesingers*.

All of these court poets were known almost exclusively for their creation of love songs. Before this time, most music had been religious or moralistic. Even the *chansons de geste* (songs of valor) of the bards bore strong religious messages and morals. But the troubadors, trouvères, minnesingers, and others developed a truly secular form of music that would lead eventually to significant changes in the profession. The trouvères were particularly noted for their secularization of the *motet*—one of the earliest forms of polyphonic music. They mixed both religious and romantic love lyrics, writing strictly in the vernacular.

The love song gave rise to a whole new class of professional musicians—notably, the minstrels. The minstrels were the ones to inherit this new secular profession because, except in Germany, the troubadors generally did not perform, but merely composed. They hired minstrels to sing or play instruments for them, in order to present their music to the court societies.

The Renaissance was a time of reviving interest in the lives, thoughts, and morals of the great heroes of Greek and Roman times. It is no surprise, then, to see the socially elite troubadors and trouvères imitating the gallant bards and epic poets of Greek times. We are not sure why they turned their work over to the minstrels for performance, but the minstrels do seem to have been more musically accomplished and often even better educated than the aristocratic poets. Many have gone so far as to label the minstrels the first truly professional musicians—either singers, instrumentalists, or both. They were certainly the first to take training in the art seriously. Between 1318 and 1447, they held annual *escoles* (minstrel schools), usually in the Low Countries. At Paris, advanced musical instruction was available. The lasting importance of the minstrel schools was to lay the foundations of an international, or at least interregional, profession of musicians that served both city and court.

The predominant image of troubadors and minstrels is one of songsters accompanying their tunes with lutes or other stringed instruments. Actually only a few especially gifted musicians sang and played an instrument at the same time. Noble households retained a good number of minstrels and other entertainers, and more commonly one would play the harp to accompany a singer. Instrumentalists seem to have been somewhat specialized by the 15th century, and players of the *troupe* or *trompette* were usually paid higher wages than other minstrels.

As for the songs themselves, the troubadors were usually the *composers*. This tradition may have set the background of a separate profession for musical composition. Still, most of the songs written were lyrics set to traditional music. As the first troubadors may have excelled in improvisational troping, those who continued in their footsteps were specialists in modifying the music of others and in creating new words for old tunes. The minstrels, meanwhile, *ad libbed* their way through even that material, so that it really became quite difficult for anyone to claim composition rights to either lyrics or melodies. In fact, before the 17th century, there were no copyright laws at all to protect original musical compositions. Anything performed or written became common property, which any other musicians could mimic or modify as they wished without regard to a composer's rights. (This was not true in all cultures; in some, composition was even sacred. For example, the Iroquois of North America were forbidden to ever again sing a song after its composer had died, since its supernatural power was thought to have been taken with him.)

To distinguish their works from those of the minstrels, some knightly troubadors began to use *trobar clus* (dark rhyming) schemes that could not be easily mimicked. Nonetheless, it was the haughty minstrel at court as well as the vagabond minstrel in the streets who kept music alive as a profession. Wherever there was entertainment, there was the minstrel. Kings and nobles sent them to fairs and religious processionals, and they provided news, popular comedy, and other entertainments— dancing, juggling, and so forth—in the streets of the new cities that had cropped up all over Western Europe by the middle of the 16th century. The troubador was almost a forgotten figure by the time feudalism dissolved and the new rich, middle-class burghers ascended to political and social prominence.

The German minnesingers were an exception to the rule of minstrels performing the music of others. They sang their own compositions and even staged elaborate contests to see whose performance was best. That tradition was later passed on to *meistersingers*, middle-class guildsmen rather than aristocrats, who flourished in the 15th and 16th centuries.

Meanwhile, as feudalism declined, court society itself waned in significance. Some of the salaried court minstrels stayed on as ministers of state and scholars, while others turned to the new forms of entertainment that the cities had to offer. In England, the *waits* (waytes) were *night watchmen* who began to group together into musical bands. Many towns dressed them handsomely and had them play at important ceremonies. It was a short-lived specialty, though, and hardly one for a serious musician. By the end of the 16th century waits were relegated to the function that they are still known for today—that of providing Christmas music in the streets of British towns. During the 16th century, the theater became the most likely place for these minstrels to find work. In 1562 there were 40 minstrels on the theater's payroll at Chelmsford, England, and only nine years later, 156 at Lucerne, Switzerland.

Changes in Music

But while professional musicians were slowly establishing their occupations in secular society, the greatest innovations in music were being undertaken by nonprofessional church musicians. In the 16th century, the polyphonic choir became a well-established form of church music, with even solo parts being sung by choral groups. Dissonance—the use of unharmonic tones to produce musical tension—and new varieties of rhythm had long since been introduced to create more interesting music, and the plainsong, with its redundant *cantus firmus*, had fallen into disuse. The greatest composers of music concentrated on new ways of altering melody and rhythm for sacred texts. Giovanni Pierluigi da Palestrina, for example, who was unrivaled in music composition in his time, wrote nothing but religious music. Church music itself led the way to more interesting musical forms. Venetian churches employed organs and two oppositional choirs singing antiphonally—that is, back and forth in response to one another. Instruments, for the first time, began to be somewhat independent of vocal music. In some instances, large churches employed professional singers, instrumentalists (mostly *organists*), and *choirmasters*. But the most obvious direct effect of sacred music on the secular profession was in the development of the *opera* and the *ricerare*, later to be called the *concert*.

The 17th and 18th centuries, with the development of the opera, the concert, and the theater, made secular music more public than it had been since the days of the Greeks. In fact, late in the 16th century, a Florentine group of singers, composers, and instrumentalists known as the Camerata had tried to re-create the status of music and song in the ancient Greek dramas. The result, combined with the influence of the Renaissance *passion plays* (staged Christian devotional dramas), was the birth of the *opera*.

At the same time, the refinement of instrumental parts in church liturgies and ceremonies had led to greater interest in purely instrumental music. The recently invented printing press had been employed in reproducing the complex musical notations necessary for the systematic distribution of instrumental pieces. Before mass printing, standardized sheet music was exceedingly rare, and musicians depended largely on vocal leads to establish melodies and rhythms. For this reason, pure instrumental music, without voices, was not easily developed, especially over time and with an increasing number of musicians performing the material.

The success of the opera made both singing and composing respectable and even laudable occupations. In its earliest years, beginning in the late 16th century, opera was chiefly a court spectacle. With the opening of the first public opera house in Venice in 1637, the dramatic,

Organists played not only in churches but also at special private affairs, such as wedding banquets. (By Jost Amman, from The Book of Trades, *late 16th century)*

spectacular type of music that common folks for centuries could hear only in church, now played on secular topics as well. Original compositions of Claudio Monteverdi and P. F. Cavalli quickly established composing as a profession of major importance, in an art form that had captured public attention and, in turn, was somewhat modified toward popular tastes.

Composers were not fully specialized, however. Monteverdi was not only a composer, but also a singer and conductor, in the same way that a century earlier another famous composer—Josquin des Prez—had also been. In fact, this pattern was commonplace in the profession even into the 18th and 19th centuries, when Wolfgang Amadeus Mozart and Ludwig von Beethoven performed as accomplished pianists, and Richard Wagner and Richard Strauss established themselves as notable conductors—all in addition to their primary careers as composers.

Singers, too, garnered public acclaim for their operatic talents. Between the 16th and 18th centuries, some boy singers were even castrated so that they would retain

Music, ballet, drama, and spectacle combined in the early operas. (Engraving by Canaletto, 1759, of Le Turc Généreux, authors' archives)

into adulthood their boyish voices, which were considered highly desirable. These so-called *castrati*—along with the principal female singers, the *prima donnas*, who became almost cult figures in the 18th century—were the prototypes of the haughty, elite, and bountifully rewarded professional singers.

Voice training became a significant feature of the occupation for the first time. Some famous singers, such as the castrato Antonio Bernacchi, founded their own private voice schools. The musical *conservatory* (specialized training school) first blossomed as a technical school for singers and composers during the Napoleonic era. The sudden rise to prominence of the conservatory was a great boon to composers and singers, and eventually to other musicians as well. It gave them not only expert professional training, but also an opportunity to work as *instructors* when they could not earn a living as performers. (In time, of course, teaching music became a profession in its own right, but even today it is still considered second to performing, among most musicians.)

Instrumentalists had received little recognition before the late 16th and 17th centuries. It was during that time that orchestras and bands of instrumentalists began to advertise public performances, the first of which was organized in 1672 by John Bannister, a violinist from London. Shortly thereafter, businessman T. Brittan sponsored a regular program of concerts that were performed for some 36 years in his coal house. Still, the most common work for concert instrumentalists was in small ensembles that performed *chamber music*—that is, private concerts in the homes of people wealthy and prestigious enough to arrange for them. Most of the larger concerts were performed for select audiences, by invitation only. The 12- to 16-member chamber orchestra of the 17th century was enlarged somewhat by the late 18th century. By the middle of the 19th it had bloomed into a full-sized symphony orchestra with often 100 or more players. Military and civil bands, meanwhile, were increasingly being employed for patriotic purposes. Napoléon was one of the first to make such use of massive band play (as well as mass choruses called the *choeurs universels*) as propaganda support.

Generally, the increase in size of orchestras and bands reflected a shift in the status of the instrumentalists from a highly elite corps, playing private chamber music for nobles and gentry, to that of public performers. Many of the 18th-century public concerts were played by amateurs, and those played by professionals were often "practice concerts." Many of Mozart's piano concertos and Beethoven's symphonies were performed as practice concerts, without any rehearsal. Changes and improvisations abounded during the course of the event. It was at this same time that the British glee club became a

Child prodigies like Mozart, here shown with his father and sister, changed the face of music. (Engraving by Delafosse after a watercolor by Carmontelle, 1763)

popular entertainment source in the same relaxed, informal tradition.

The casual attitude of the profession toward its audience had its roots in two facts. First, not until the 19th-century Industrial Revolution did the general population have the time, money, or opportunity to hear musical spectacles outside of the church; and musicians accustomed to playing exclusively for nobility were little awed by middle-class merchants, much less laborers. Second, the audience did not intend to merely listen to a concert. People smoked their pipes, played cards, chatted with one another, and otherwise amused themselves. The orchestral music, whether in a hall or on a green, was purely incidental to the festivities.

The most prestigious of the instrumentalists was the *soloist*, who could give an entire concert alone. Performing as solo pianists, violinists, and so forth, many fine composers gained the financial independence to continue composing. Other soloists were purely instrumentalists; they might perform either as soloists or as orchestra members.

By the time coal was turning the world of genteel trade and commerce into one of muscle-and-grit manufacturing, musicians had become respected professionals. Master composers and solo instrumentalists were being granted honorary doctorates from universities, conservatories, and *collegia musica*. Great musicians like Georg Friedrich Handel and Beethoven, and even lesser ones, achieved the status of *professor of music* by virtue of their accomplishments; others received papal decorations and even noble titles. This did not necessarily imply financial stability. Many were dependent on uncertain patronage and died, like Mozart, in poverty. Even in the wilds of America, where culture was not known to thrive, both vocal and instrumental concerts became a way of life in untypically aristocratic Charleston by the time of the American Revolution. That same city founded the St. Cecilia Society, the first paid municipal orchestra in the New World. Still, the growth of large cities and the rise of the laboring class gave great impetus to new forms of popular—as opposed to *classical*—music. Musicians thereby found new markets for their skills; but at the same time, popular musicians commanded little respect and were frequently despised.

The theater was the greatest source of advancement for popular musicians. In the 18th and 19th centuries, the *Singspiel* (Beggar's Opera) had appeared as a common man's simplified version of "legitimate" or "court" opera. Singspiel troupes hit the road all across Europe, attracting large numbers of followers. By the second half of the 19th century these troupes were presenting *operettas*—even more colloquial and lighter still than the Singspiel—with great success in Vienna and Paris. At the same time, *variety shows* in London, New York, and other big cities were reviving the specialty of the minstrel. *Vaudeville* and *burlesque theaters* throughout the Western world provided numerous—if not necessarily lucrative or appealing—opportunities for musicians, dancers, singers, magicians, and other performers. Many of the new "minstrels" had little musical training or knowledge; they were often drawn from the lower classes, and even included women and Blacks (especially in America). Even *music rooms* in London taverns and American frontier saloons offered some opportunities for those wishing to peddle their musical talents. The English *music hall* did the same on a grander scale. Before the 20th century, all of these musical "theaters" featured music and song only incidentally, though. Primarily, they showcased comedy and drama skits, with music only filling in some dead time between the main acts. Musicians in these situations were well-advised to be actors as well, if they were to avoid starvation.

The 20th-century Musician

The 20th century saw all of these theater forms refined to include *variety entertainment*. At the turn of the century and even into World War II the music halls and the vaudeville and burlesque theaters in Europe and America featured a broad range of short entertainment pieces that tended to favor music over drama. Meanwhile, by the 1920's, the theater itself came to absorb music into its format. New York's Broadway musical shows, which are still a unique entertainment form today, set the pace for this new merger of music with drama and comedy. In many ways performers in these Broadway musicals were akin to opera and operetta singers and musicians. However—this form of entertainment being more typically American—they had much closer ties to the *showboat performers* and *black-face minstrels* of earlier generations who had danced, acted, joked, and sung their way along the rivers and highways of the new land.

The greatest impact on the musical professions has been the 20th-century development of radio, television, movies, records, and more recently, video cassettes and video discs. These media quickly replaced most live music shows, leaving popular singers with only a few regular showcases—cabarets, night clubs, cafes, and bars. The most successful popular performers, of course, can regularly fill large concert halls. Classical musicians have been far less affected; although there is a market for classical recordings, there is also considerable emphasis on regularly scheduled live performances by symphony orchestras, opera companies, and solo classical musicians.

All musicians, though, have been affected by massive trends in popularity and taste, and by the need to "catch" an anonymous public with a certain image or sound that—once recorded—will be reproduced hundreds of thousands, or even millions of times over. Because of the enormous expense involved, record companies and radio stations tend to present only the works of those singers or instrumentalists whom they feel most certain will be accepted, usually because of a proven track record—a well-known name. The results have been that a handful of recording stars and groups tend to dominate the "rock" and "pop" music industry, which financially represents the most successful sectors of the music profession today. The vast number of other musicians work the cafes or the streets, waiting for a chance that seldom comes. So, there is often a sameness to the music offered to the public over a given period of time, since *promoters* rather than the actual performers tend to determine what should be offered or recorded.

Women and minorities have often had difficulty breaking into musical careers in established fields. Although women singers have long been popular, female instrumentalists have seldom been accepted easily, either in popular or classical music. Even as late as 1984, a major international orchestra, the Berlin Philharmonic, had a major dispute with its conductor, Herbert von Karajan, over the hiring of a female clarinetist.

Segregated from much of White culture, Blacks in the 20th century developed their own distinctive music—blues and jazz. These have had enormous influence on all forms of modern music. Ironically, Whites often came to take the forms as their own, excluding Blacks from their orchestras or instrumental groups.

The musical profession is far more complex now than ever before. Beer-garden concerts and practice concerts, private chamber recitals and showcase cabarets are rare today. Opera, musical theater, and formal concerts are still very much alive, of course, but performing in these traditional forms is also more complex than in past times. If nothing else, there are musicians' unions, municipal contracts, and *agents'* agreements to consider. The electric media created the "rock" generation, which developed its own standard types of musicians— younger, brasher, and less conventional.

Yet some basic things have remained fairly constant. As always, musicians provide a luxury art and entertainment that people are willing to pay for. However, there is still keen competition to be among the few who have the good fortune to be accepted in the field. For each successful and comfortable musician, there are many who work little clubs, or worse yet, have to find other types of employment altogether, while continually seeking the elusive opportunity for professional success.

The music professions include a wide variety of specialties. A monk named Guido d'Arezzo in the 11th century A.D. was the first person to use a graphic system of music notation to record and preserve pieces of music he had created. It was several hundred years later before the printing press made such a system practical on a large scale. *Musical copyists* did—and still do—the actual writing of musical scores. In earlier times com-

In modern times, singers like Pete Seeger have become celebrities and had considerable influence on their times. (By Arthur Rothstein, from The Depression Years, *Dover, 1978; American Youth Congress, 1940)*

posers often worked as their own copyists. Modern musical copyists more often work from rough notations, usually adaptations made by *arrangers* and *orchestrators*. While composers create new musical themes, scores, and songs, arrangers and orchestrators typically adapt existing pieces to particular uses, arranging musical scores for instrumentalists and vocalists in choral or orchestral groups or bands. Frequently they "re-arrange" such pieces in the process. People have employed their talents in these ways for many centuries, but as strict specializations, the occupations are fairly modern.

Conductors and *chorus directors* are elite specialists in music. Symphony orchestras were not very popular until the middle of the 19th century. The occupation of conductor is therefore a fairly modern one. Choirs and choruses, though, have their roots in Greek drama, so choral music directors have a much longer history. For many centuries they were the choirmasters of the church and of the parish schools. Many still function in that capacity today, although the profession has also been secularized to a great extent.

The conductor leads symphonies or bands—any large groups of instrumentalists. The chorus director or choirmaster leads large groups of vocalists. Conductors must be adept in all phases of instrumental music, since the quality of the final performance is left to their discretion and direction. Besides understanding the actual technique of conducting, conductors are also responsible for choosing and sometimes even rearranging music that best fits the talents and scope of the group under their direction. Conductors must be thoroughly familiar with the individual characteristics of each instrument in the band or orchestra, in order to effect the desired rhythm, tempo, and overall harmony. Choral directors must know how to bring many various voices together into harmony. While conductors and choral directors must be well trained in musical theory, they are primarily public performers. The finished product and the resulting audience and critical reaction spell success or failure for conductors, and they must be willing to cope with that reality.

Recording acoustic engineers and *sound technicians* are very recent occupations, since the recording of music is barely half a century old. There are many technical specialties within this broad category. *Sound mixers* monitor the volume and quality of recorded sound, and are responsible for the proper blending of all sounds recorded. The *re-recording mixer* combines several sound tracks into one final, finished product, while the *recordist* operates the recording machines. These occupations are highly technical, requiring considerable background and training in sound theory and technical sound engineering. Employment opportunities for qualified professionals are found in radio, television, movie, record, and tape studios.

Music *teachers* have worked professionally ever since the days of ancient Greece, if not earlier. The profession was a fairly insignificant and unorganized one, though, until music was introduced into the public school curriculum in the 19th and 20th centuries. The profession then drifted away from the clerics who had taught music in the parish and cathedral schools for centuries. Instead, many lay (non-church) musicians found employment as *teachers* in public schools. Today, music teachers must be well trained in both musical theory and educational methods. They find employment at all levels of education, and many work independently as private tutors.

For related occupations in this volume, *Performers and Players*, see the following:
    Actors
    Athletes
    Dancers
    Puppeteers
    Variety Performers

For related occupations in other volumes of the series, see the following:
in *Communicators*:
    Authors
    Printers
    Scribes
in *Healers* (forthcoming):
    Physicians and Surgeons
in *Helpers and Aides*:

Private Guards and Detectives
Servants and Other Domestic Laborers
Undertakers
in *Leaders and Lawyers*:
Political Leaders
in *Restaurateurs and Innkeepers* (forthcoming):
Innkeepers
Prostitutes
Restaurateurs
in *Scholars and Priests*:
Monks and Nuns
Priests
Scholars
Teachers
in *Scientists and Technologists*:
Mathematicians
Physicists
in *Warriors and Adventurers*:
Soldiers

Puppeteers

Puppeteering has been an honored profession in the Far East since early history. Originally, it had considerable religious significance, since the majority of puppet shows were designed to instruct the audience in proper moral conduct and even philosophical understanding. Shadow play theaters, dating back to at least the second century B.C., were as popular as puppet shows. Both *puppeteers* and the closely associated *shadow players* were thought to possess nearly mystical powers. The figures they created and operated were regarded as materializations of divinities and deceased souls. The puppeteers themselves were seen as *magicians, spiritual mediums,* and *shamans.*

In the Western world, puppeteers also had early ties to temple and cultic rituals. Egyptian priests apparently developed a regular puppet theater that was used in funeral ceremonies to invoke the presence of departed souls and to seek the guidance and favor of the gods. Greek *string-pullers* and Roman puppeteers also had some place in ritual and sacred gatherings. Theater itself, though, was dominated by *actors* who wore masks to convey various roles and emotions—in a sense mimicking the puppets. After the disintegration of the Roman Empire, puppeteers largely disappeared from Europe for a time.

Hindu puppeteers seem to have been the first of their profession to develop puppetry and shadow play as entertainment forms. The first purely professional puppeteers seem to have emerged as a class separate from *wizards, magicians*, and *priests*, who had developed the art as an appendage to their various callings. Even as entertainers, though, Eastern puppeteers continued to work out themes of morality and social obligation.

The status of puppeteers remained highly honorable, particularly in China and Japan. They were regarded as first-rate *artists* and *teachers* who played an important role in society. *Emperors* patronized them and retained them in high positions at court. They also dominated the more worldly scene of theatrical display. During the Sung dynasty of the 10th through 13th centuries, they were extremely prominent figures at the popular *teahouses*, as well as in the puppet and shadow play theaters. They worked in troupes or one-person shows, dramatizing traditional stories and themes of morality. Outside of the flourishing theater and entertainment districts of China and Japan, puppeteers were wanderers in search of patronage and audiences. Oe Tadafusa's *Book of Puppeteers*, published around 100 A.D., was the first to present the life and work of the professional puppeteer.

In Islamic society, the making of images such as puppets was forbidden by law. Shadow theater became a highly polished art in place of pure puppetry. The

Puppeteers often used assistants standing out in front, like this drummer, to help catch the audience's attention. (From Advertising Woodcuts From the Nineteenth-Century Stage, *by Stanley Appelbaum, Dover, 1977)*

Mexicans and Native Americans also developed shadow theater, using flat figures to cast opaque silhouettes.

The medieval church revived puppetry in the West, particularly in Italy and France. Initially, *priests* and *clerics* used puppets to stage Christian morality plays at chapel schools. By the 16th century, though, puppets were banned from the church itself. A secular class of puppeteers continued the tradition. They performed religious themes and miracle plays at festivals and on street corners.

Gradually, puppeteers developed more secular and comical, even satirical and political, themes. The very popular puppet *Polcinella* of Renaissance Italy was a character of high Christian virtue and morality. As *Polichinelle* in France, he became less austere, however. And by the time he arrived in London in the 1660's as "Punch," he was quite a different sort of character. "Punch and Judy" were a rowdy and worldly husband and wife who fought with each other and displayed crude manners and violence, to the delight of the mobs of children and adults who attended their performances. The puppeteer was usually a man who sat in a tall, thin, boxlike showcase, raising his arms to display his characters, while he remained hidden. He did the vocals, and a hired *drummer* or *flutist* often stood outside the box to provide added theatrics.

Western puppeteers developed considerable flexibility and popularity with their characters. In Venice, *marionettes* (stringed puppets) were the rage of the 17th century. In France, puppeteers performed full-scale operas and Eastern-style shadow theater productions. Shadow theater using silhouettes was popular in European court society and Colonial America as parlor entertainment by the 18th century. In England, puppeteers became highly political and controversial. In the 18th and 19th centuries, puppets were a major attraction all over Europe and in America. Munich had two established puppet theaters, one traditional and one experimental to encourage further development in the profession of puppetry.

Lewis Carroll and Hans Christian Andersen were among the numerous noted writers who made their own puppets to dramatize their works. Many writers hired puppeteers to showcase their stories. American fairs, circuses, and city street corners were filled with the bustle of competing puppeteers. European and American puppeteers did not rival their Eastern counterparts in artistry, professional development, or socioeconomic status, however. They were always more on a par with the generally despised stage actor, and their lives were more typically characterized by wandering and meager rewards.

Eastern puppeteers reached great heights in their profession with the establishment of the *doll theater*. Both Tokyo and Osaka had regular doll theater companies by 1685. While early puppeteers used only the heads of dolls, hands and feet were later added, and eventually whole bodies were used. Working these dolls demanded tremendous skill, as moving joints, eyes, and even eyebrows were added. Puppeteers to operate Eastern doll theaters were in great demand during the 18th century. By 1750, each doll required three operators: one to move the head and right arm, one to move the left arm, and one to move the feet. By this time, the figures stood about 3 or 4 feet high, and their operators were seated on center stage, in full view of the audience. The handlers were to develop emotion and character, much like modern actors. Their training was intense. Some 10 years were required to master the operation of the feet, and another 10 years for the operation of the left hand. Only then could one study head and right-arm operation. It is little wonder that Eastern puppeteers were regarded with awe and respect as first-rate artists.

In the 20th century, Western puppeteers have played increasingly within the confines of children's theater. Television gave rise to a series of popular puppet shows for children, starring such puppet characters as Burr Tillstrom's Kukla, Fran, and Ollie; Paul Winchell's Jerry Mahoney; Howdy Doody; and most recently Jim Henson's Muppets, of *Sesame Street* fame. Many puppeteers working in cabarets developed considerable skills as *ventriloquists*. Edgar Bergen, for example, displayed great skill in seemingly giving life to his famous *dummy*, Charlie McCarthy.

In the East, the profession is still a more austere and respected one for the most part. Adults as well as children attend puppet theaters, which produce dramatic as well as comical productions. Professional expertise still tends to be far greater in the East, as it has always been. On Java in Indonesia, for instance, one puppeteer is charged with handling some 300 to 400 leather cut-out puppets (the *Wayang Kulit*) during the traditional shadow play that lasts from 8:30 P.M. until dawn. During this marathon production, he not only operates the figures, but also provides the narrative, the sound effects, and the music and song, even improvising the dialogue.

For related occupations in this volume, *Performers and Players*, see the following:
  Actors
  Musicians
  Variety Performers

For related occupations in other volumes of the series, see the following:
in *Helpers and Aides*:
  Undertakers
in *Leaders and Lawyers*:
  Political Leaders
in *Restaurateurs and Innkeepers* (forthcoming):
  Innkeepers
  Restaurateurs
in *Scholars and Priests*:
  Priests
  Teachers

Racers

Automobile racers were first employed in France in 1894, and in the United States the following year. *Rowers* have raced each other for prizes since at least the 16th century, when Henry VIII of England demanded the licensing of oarsmen for the sake of water safety on the Thames River. There are also professional *motorboat, sailboat,* and *yacht racers,* among others. All these racers have one feature in common: they do not engage in contests that primarily and directly test their physical prowess. They are considered less *athletes* than *sport performers* using some intermediary, such as a boat, a horse, or an automobile.

In ancient times, before horses were common, racing did not exist as a profession. When horses began to be used for war, they were also employed in racing.

Warriors were probably the first professional *jockeys*, or *riders*. As the machine age propelled humanity into modern times, automobiles began to replace horses in most ways, and automobile racing became as popular as horse racing.

Different qualities are specific to various types of racing. For instance, automobile racers are employed in a very risky business, much as the ancient *charioteers* were. And oarsmen, who today are typically amateurs, are more physically involved in their sport than other racers usually are. We will take the example of the *horse racer* as a model for racing as an occupation, because it is the most historically developed.

Horse racers have existed since the days of ancient Assyria, dating back to at least 1500 B.C. Horse racing was popular in the ancient East from China to Persia, and good riders were undoubtedly held in high regard. But in ancient Rome, where the sport reached the height of its popularity, it seems that the horses were given at least equal regard. They had "proper" burials, and on their graves were inscribed monuments that recalled their record of victories. One such monument bore an impressive record of 1,300 "career"victories, as well as 88 seconds and 37 thirds.

Ancient riders were often of high social standing, especially related to their military ranking. This was particularly notable in Rome, where most athletes were *slaves*, hirelings, or foreigners. Apparently, the sport attracted high-status individuals because it had a somewhat practical and elite tradition. Roman riders, like their horses, had all of their accomplishments recorded in terms of wins, seconds, and thirds. These records were used to rank riders among their peers and were, therefore, very important.

After the fall of Rome, horse racing apparently died out as a significant sport, as religious asceticism and feudalism gave people other things to devote their time to—like saving their souls and working the fields. Richard the Lion-Hearted, king of England, revived the sport in the 12th century when he purchased fleet-footed Arabian horses and later offered the first prize for a race in which *knights* were the riders. This seems reasonable, since knights—as the main "performers" in the medieval tournaments—had to be excellent horsemen.

In the early Middle Ages most horse races were *match races*. That is, two horse owners would put up money to bet that one horse was faster than the other. A "winner-takes-the-pot" race would ensue. These races were favorite events at medieval fairs. Prizes were not offered to winners until 1512 though, when a wooden ball—probably the first racing trophy—was awarded by the promoters of the annual British fair at Chester, a famous racing center. Soon after that, silver and gold balls replaced wooden ones, and professional racing had begun. In the early 18th century, Queen Anne of England initiated the horse-racing sweepstakes.

Since match racing of horses in England was a favorite sport of British royalty, it is not surprising that most of the riders would be gentlemen of high social standing. As the sport spread to the American Colonies, it remained a sport for the elite. Fines were occasionally levied upon commoners who were caught racing their horses against those of gentlemen planters. The match races of earlier days were made obsolete in the late 17th century when field racing replaced them. The match races had usually featured the two horse owners riding their own horses. Many a rider failed to show, however, and "play or pay" rules had to be initiated so that the delinquent racer would forfeit his half of the purse to his opponent. This did not please the spectators or bettors who had gathered for the event, though, and field racing came into vogue.

Field racing opened up the profession considerably because it featured an entry sheet of many horses so that, if one or two forfeited, the race could still take place. As many owners had many horses, and often wished to enter several in one or more races, they had to hire riders to do what they used to do. Professional riders were not new, but they now had greater opportunities. As gentlemen were more critical of hired riders than they were of themselves, skilled riders were sought more eagerly and their social standing became less important than their horsemanship.

Horse racing had begun to become more organized. Even in the New World, New York Governor Frank Lovelace sponsored a sweepstake race as early as 1669 at Newmarket Course. The prize was two silver cups. In 1751 the first British horsemen's association, the still-famous Jockey Club, was formed by wealthy breeders and owners to set guidelines and more exact rules for future races. Even today the rulings of the Jockey Club are generally considered the world's authority on the sport and its proceedings.

Racers have always been at risk, as here at the Tattenham Corner of Britain's Derby. (By Gustave Doré, from London: A Pilgrimage, *1872)*

There was still considerable sentiment that it was the horse and not the rider that ran the winning race. As a result there was not always a great deal of competition for the position of *jockey*, as these horse riders came to be called. When the Kentucky Derby opened in the late 19th century, almost all the jockeys were Blacks. *Bookmakers* hit the track scene in 1873, though, and the horse started earning too much money to overlook any aspect of the race. Highly competitive North-South races offered rich purses, so better-qualified jockeys were eagerly sought. As jockeys received both higher pay and greater status, Blacks were pushed out of the profession altogether and White professional riders entered the field.

Horse racing today is a sophisticated game of skill and numbers. Enormous sums ride on each race, and jockeys have assumed a central role in the failures and successes of the horses. Accordingly, they are also a highly paid class of professionals who, in the last 50 years, have attained unprecedented glory, credit, and status for their successes.

For related occupations in this volume, *Performers and Players*, see the following:
    Athletes

For related occupations in other volumes of the series, see the following:
in *Helpers and Aides*:
    Drivers
in *Warriors and Adventurers*:
    Gamblers and Gamesters
    Soldiers

Variety Performers

Acrobats, rope walkers, mimes, clowns, jugglers, magicians, fortune-tellers, animal trainers, strong men, large women, little people—all these and more have worked as *variety performers* during the course of human history. They have also been variously called *circus people, vaudevillians, music-hall performers, joculators, jongleurs, minstrels, harlequins, zanies, beast baiters, bareback riders, mountebanks, fools, jesters, escape artists, contortionists, freaks, conjurors,* and *trapeze artists.*

Three thousand years ago, in China, they were known as the people of the "hundred plays." In Greece, they were working in traveling troupes as early as the seventh century B.C. In India, they were playing the comedy role in Sanskrit drama 2,000 years ago. In Rome, they were

Variety performers like these Japanese jugglers and acrobats have been popular in East Asia for many centuries. (From Advertising Woodcuts From the Nineteenth-Century Stage, by Stanley Appelbaum, Dover, 1977)

travelers, as they had been in Greece. They were precursors of the performers who took to the European road after the fall of Rome, and stayed on the road for hundreds of years. In Byzantium—the Eastern Roman Empire—they were the same, but with more ability to work in the centers of population.

During the Renaissance, they continued to travel, working at fairs, festivals, carnivals, and pageants. During the modern period, some moved into a relatively fixed form, the *circus*, while others traveled with carnivals and worked in such forms as vaudeville and music hall. These were some of the most popular performing artists, their work appealing to mass populations far more than the work of the leading *theater artists* of their times. No *dramatists* wrote directly for them, and until the modern period the historical record relating to them is very modest indeed.

In the post-Renaissance Western theater, most *actors, dancers,* and *singers* have moved into the major artistic forms of the modern period—the spoken theater, ballet, modern dance, and opera, live and on screen. But the other artists with whom they traveled the roads of Europe in medieval and Renaissance times have remained together, in troupes, much like those of older times, although mightily assisted by modern techniques and machinery. In the last two and a half centuries, they have played in carnivals and fairs, and continue to do so in the 20th century. In the last century, still traveling, they played in vaudeville and music hall, working as variety acts side by side with the star popular entertainers of the time. To a limited extent they continue to do so in the 20th century in such places as Las Vegas night clubs and on television stages.

The most sustained, rounded continuation of the traveling performing artist-troupe tradition, which stretches back to the Dorian Greeks, is the modern circus. Here are to be found all the artists of the traveling troupes, in many cases working much as they did in earlier times, and with over 2,500 years of artistic tradition and skills development behind them.

The modern circus owes the name of its form and the idea of working in an arena to the Greeks and Romans. The Romans called their version of the Greek *hippodrome* a circus. The Circus Maximus in Rome was a somewhat oval-shaped combination of racetrack and sporting arena, ultimately capable of seating between 200,000 and 250,000 people.

The Roman circus featured chariot racing, virtuoso displays of horsemanship, animal baiting (which was the forerunner of modern bullfighting), and a substantial variety of sideshows featuring the acts of the traveling players of the ancient world—jugglers, acrobats, rope walkers, and weight lifters among them. Many of the performing artists working in the Roman circus—and in the Roman theater altogether—were *slaves*, who had gained their skills in Greece and other Mediterranean countries.

The modern circus is not a revival of the Roman circus. Rather, it is a continuation of a popular entertainment tradition and set of skills going back over 2,500 years. The other major art forms enjoyed a Renaissance—that is, they had to be revived after having died out for a time. The popular arts merely continued, serving as an underlying base of theater and theater people upon which the Renaissance could grow.

Throughout the Middle Ages, professional artists, most of them from Italy and other southern European areas, toured in variety troupes. These included acrobats, jugglers, jesters or clowns, conjurors, freaks, animal trainers and exhibitors, rope walkers, and trick riders. The consummate professionals working in the servants' roles in *commedia dell'arte* acting companies originated the roles of Harlequin and Pierrot, the archetypes of the modern professional clown. All the other artists continued to work and develop the skills that were eventually to be transferred and continued in the circus companies of the 18th century.

Charles Astley, a skilled trick rider, is generally credited with being the originator of the modern circus. In 1768, on leaving the army, he and his wife set up a riding school and performing ring at a field named Halfpenny Hatch, south of Westminster Bridge in London. His riding ring was an important innovation, for it literally gave shape to the circus movement that followed. Astley and those who followed found that riding in a ring took advantage of centrifugal force, holding rider and horse together more effectively than had been possible earlier.

By 1780, Astley was able to set up a permanent structure, the prototype of the circus buildings that were to follow. It consisted of a large open ring surrounded by covered grandstands. In that structure, the first modern circus building, he presented acrobats, slackrope and tightrope walkers, a dog trainer exhibiting dancing dogs, and his own trick riders, all working in and around the ring. So the modern circus company was born, composed of performers who had been working in the popular variety theater all along. He added many acts in the next two years, and by 1782, when he took his troupe to Paris for the first time, it included most of the kinds of artists working in the variety theater of the time.

In 1782, Astley encountered competition, in the form of a new London troupe organized by Charles Hughes, one of his former riders. The new troupe used the word *circus* in its title for the first time in the modern period. It was named the Royal Circus, although it was a purely private organization, with no hint of official support or subsidy.

The Astley and Hughes troupes were permanently headquartered, as were many of the European troupes that were to follow. In 1792, Astley was forced to flee France because of the war between France and England. He left his permanent circus building in Paris to his co-worker, Antonio Franconi. Franconi is regarded as the founder of the French circus. He was the first of four generations of Franconis, the leading family in the French circus for a century.

John Bill Ricketts, who had been a pupil of Charles Hughes in England, opened the first American circus in 1793 in Philadelphia. This, too, was a permanent structure. By the middle of the 18th century, the circus was established as a growing entertainment institution throughout Europe and North America, with permanent circus companies headquartered in many major cities.

At the same time, the tradition of the traveling company continued. Ultimately it was to dominate American

To drum up support for their shows, players often held parades through the streets, giving samples of their diverse entertainments. (From Punch, *or* The London Charivari)

and British circus practice. By the late 18th century, Thomas Cooke's British traveling company had essentially transformed itself into a small circus, starting a major British circus family. In the United States, Hachaliah Bailey bought an elephant in 1815, and profited greatly by going on the road, with the elephant as a one-animal menagerie. By the 1830's, the traveling menagerie was an established part of the American scene. Also in the United States, Aron Turner in 1830 solved the problem of presenting a traveling circus outdoors by taking his circus on tour under a tent. His was the first *big top*, the form that was to characterize the traveling American circus from then on. This was the beginning of a style of presentation that ultimately would be able to seat more than 10,000 people at once under a circus tent—the Big Top of the Ringling Brothers Barnum and Bailey Circus.

In the 19th and early 20th centuries, some circus performers in Western Europe and America were great popular stars. The French tightrope walker Emilie Gravelet, known as Blondin, captured extraordinary attention by walking across Niagara Falls on a wire suspended high over the falls in 1859. He was to repeat the feat on several occasions. The French acrobat Léotard invented the trapeze in the same year. That most extraordinary professional pantomimist, Joseph Grimaldi, decisively turned the clown's art toward identification with the silent harlequin. All circus clowns after him would be known by the generic name "Joey." In the 20th century, only the American clown Emmett Kelly and the Russian clown Oleg Popov have achieved anything like the popular acclaim of the 19th-century circus stars.

Toward the latter part of the 20th century, many large circuses have abandoned the road and—as in the 18th century—now only play in great permanent structures, such as New York City's Madison Square Garden. But some smaller tent circuses—called *mud shows*—still travel from town to town. And many a young boy or girl—indeed, many an adult—still longs to run away and join the circus.

For related occupations in this volume, *Performers and Players*, see the following:
   Actors
   Athletes
   Dancers
   Musicians
   Puppeteers
   Racers

For related occupations in other volumes of the series, see the following:
in *Scientists and Technologists*:
   Astrologers

Suggestions for Further Reading

For further information about the occupations in this family, you may wish to consult the books below.

Actors and Puppeteers

Appia, Adolphe. *The Work of Living Art*. Miami, Florida: University of Miami Press, 1960. Translated by H.D. Albright. A basic theoretical work on theater and theater design.

Arlington, Lewis C. *The Chinese Drama from the Earliest Times to Today*. Bronx, New York: B. Blom, 1966. A useful review.

Arnott, Peter D. *The Ancient Greek and Roman Theatre*. New York: Random House, 1971. A helpful review.

Baker, Michael. *The Rise of the Victorian Actor*. London: Rowman & Littlefield, 1978.

Berthold, Margot. *A History of World Theatre*. New York: Frederick Ungar, 1972. A standard, well-illustrated work translated from the German.

Bharata Muni. *Natya-Sastra*. Calcutta: Manisha Gran Thalia, 1961. In 2 vols. Translated by Manmohan Ghosh. A basic treatise on Indian theater.

Bowers, Faubian. *Japanese Theatre*. New York: Hermitage, 1952. An informative, interesting guide through the history of Japanese dance, puppetry, and drama.

Brockett, Oscar G. *History of the Theatre*. Boston, Massachusetts: Allyn and Bacon, 1977. A very useful standard work.

Cheney, Sheldon. *The Theatre*. New York: McKay, 1952. A basic work, with a good bibliography.

Cole, Toby, and Helen K. Chinoy. *Actors on Acting*. New York: Crown, 1949. A useful firsthand view.

Craig, Edward Gordon. *The Art of the Theatre*. London: T.N. Foulis, 1905.

———. *Towards a New Theatre*. London: J.M. Dent, 1913.

———. *The Theatre Advancing*. Boston, Massachusetts: Little, Brown, 1919. Basic theoretical and practical works on modern theater and theater design.

Ernst, Earle. *Kabuki Theatre*. New York: Grove Press, 1956.

Freedley, George, and John A. Reeves. *A History of the Theatre*. New York: Crown, 1968. A standard and useful work.

Gascoigne, Bamber. *World Theatre: An Illustrated History*. Boston, Massachusetts: Little, Brown, 1968. A standard work with excellent illustrations.

Geisinger, Marion. *Plays, Players, and Playwrights*. New York: 1975. A standard work.

Gilder, Rosamund. *Enter the Actress*. New York: Theatre Arts, 1961. Useful on women in acting.

Hartnoll, Phyllis. *A Concise History of the Theatre*. London: Thames, 1968. A good standard work.

Macgowan, Kenneth, and William Melnitz. *The Living Stage*. Englewood Cliffs, New Jersey: Prentice-Hall, 1955. A standard work.

Mantzius, Karl. *A History of Theatrical Art*. New York: Peter Smith, 1937; reprint of 1904 6-vol. ed. A standard older work, with excellent detail, but questionable analysis.

Molinari, Cesar. *Theatre Through the Ages*. New York: McGraw-Hill, 1975. A basic general work.

Mongédian, Georges. *Daily Life in the French Theatre at the Time of Molière*. London: Allen and Unwin, 1969. Useful for social detail.

Nicoll, Allardyce. *The Development of the Theatre*. New York: Harcourt, Brace, 1963.

——. *Masks, Mimes, and Miracles: Studies in the Popular Theatre*. New York: Burns & McEachern, 1963. Both basic and useful works.

Scott, A.C. *The Classical Theatre of China*. London: Allen and Unwin, 1957. A basic work.

——. *Kabuki Theatre of Japan*. London: Allen and Unwin, 1955. A useful work.

Stanislavsky, Konstantin S. *An Actor Prepares*. New York: Theatre Arts, 1936.

——. *My Life in Art*. Boston, Massachusetts: Little, Brown, 1938. A basic work in modern acting history.

Wilson, Garff A. *A History of American Acting*. Indianapolis, Indiana: Indiana University Press, 1966. A useful overview.

Athletes, Gamblers, and Racers

Ball, Donald W., and John W. Loy. *Sport and the Social Order: Contributions to the Sociology of Sport*. Reading, Massachusetts: Addison-Wesley, 1975. Offers interesting insight into the social consequences of the athletic profession.

Cashman, Richard, and Michael McKernan, eds. *Sport in History*. New York: University of Queensland Press, 1979. A good, general history of sports and its key figures.

Gardiner, E. Norman. *Athletics of the Ancient World*. Chicago, Illinois: Ares Publications, 1978. An excellent overview of the history of sports and athletes, clearly showing the general movement of athletics from amateurism toward professionalism.

Guttman, Allen. *From Ritual to Record: The Nature of Modern Sports.* New York: Columbia University Press, 1979. A readable, intellectual analysis of the increasing sophistication of sports, and the changing role of the athlete in society.

Higgs, Robert J., and Neil D. Isaacs. *The Sporting Spirit: Athletes in Literature and Life.* San Diego, California: Harcourt, Brace, Jovanovich, 1977. Athletes come to life in this close-up view of the participants who have helped shape this profession.

Manchester, Herbert. *Four Centuries of Sports in America: 1490-1890.* Salem, New Hampshire: Ayer, 1968. A colorful look at athletic heroes and the rise of professionalism in American sports.

Noll, Roger G., ed. *Government and the Sport Business.* Washington, D.C.: Brookings Institution, 1974. Athletes are viewed here as businesspeople more than "players"; gives a keen perspective of sport as big business.

Zeigler, Earle F., ed. *History of Physical Education and Sport.* Englewood Cliffs, New Jersey: Prentice-Hall, 1979. An interesting analysis of the role of sport and athletes in the realm of education.

Directors

Cole, Toby, and Helen K. Chinoy. *Directors on Directing.* Indianapolis, Indiana: Bobbs-Merrill, 1963. A quite useful work.

Dancers

Bland, Alexander. *A History of Ballet and Dance.* New York: Praeger, 1976. A general work.

Clarke, Mary and Clement Crisp. *The History of Dance.* New York: Crown, 1981. A well-illustrated modern work, covering East as well as West.

Haskell, Arnold Lionel. *Ballet.* Harmondsworth, England: Penguin, 1938. A British work.

Kirstein, Lincoln. *Dance: A Short History of Classic Theatrical Dancing.* New York: Dance Horizons, 1969. A standard work.

Kraus, Richard. *History of the Dance.* Englewood Cliffs, New Jersey: Prentice-Hall, 1969. A standard general work.

Lawler, Lillian B. *The Dance in Ancient Greece.* Toronto, Canada: Macmillan, 1964. A useful standard work.

Lawson, Joan. *A History of Ballet and Its Makers.* London: Pitman, 1964. A useful standard work.

Sachs, Kurt. *World History of the Dance.* New York: Norton Publishers, 1978. An overview of all dance forms around the world.

Singha, Rina, and Reginald Massey. *Indian Dances: Their History and Growth.* New York: Braziller, 1967. An interesting look at some Eastern dance forms and dancers, with good historical background.

Index